6. Enter your class ID code to join a class.

IF YOU HAVE A CLASS CODE FROM YOUR TEACHER

a. Enter your class code and click [Next]

b. Once you have joined a class, you will be able to use the Discussion Board and Email tools.

c. To enter this code later, choose **Join a Class**.

IF YOU DO NOT HAVE A CLASS CODE

a. If you do not have a class ID code, click [Skip]

b. You do not need a class ID code to use *iQ Online*.

c. To enter this code later, choose **Join a Class**.

7. Review registration information and click Log In. Then choose your book. Click **Activities** to begin using *iQ Online*.

IMPORTANT

- After you register, the next time you want to use *iQ Online*, go to www.iQOnlinePractice.com and log in with your email address and password.
- The online content can be used for 12 months from the date you register.
- For help, please contact customer service: eltsupport@oup.com.

WHAT IS iQ ONLINE ?

All new activities provide essential skills **practice** and support.

Vocabulary and Grammar **games** immerse you in the language and provide even more practice.

Authentic, engaging **videos** generate new ideas and opinions on the Unit Question.

Go to the Media Center to download or stream all **student book audio**.

Use the **Discussion Board** to discuss the Unit Question and more.

Email encourages communication with your teacher and classmates.

Automatic grading gives immediate feedback and tracks progress.

Progress Reports show what you have mastered and where you still need more practice.

SHAPING learning TOGETHER

We would like to acknowledge the teachers from all over the world who participated in the development process and review of the Q series.

Special thanks to our *Q: Skills for Success* Second Edition Topic Advisory Board

Shaker Ali Al-Mohammad, Buraimi University College, Oman; **Dr. Asmaa A. Ebrahim**, University of Sharjah, U.A.E.; **Rachel Batchilder**, College of the North Atlantic, Qatar; **Anil Bayir**, Izmir University, Turkey; **Flora Mcvay Bozkurt**, Maltepe University, Turkey; **Paul Bradley**, University of the Thai Chamber of Commerce Bangkok, Thailand; **Joan Birrell-Bertrand**, University of Manitoba, MB, Canada; **Karen E. Caldwell**, Zayed University, U.A.E.; **Nicole Hammond Carrasquel**, University of Central Florida, FL, U.S.; **Kevin Countryman**, Seneca College of Applied Arts & Technology, ON, Canada; **Julie Crocker**, Arcadia University, NS, Canada; **Marc L. Cummings**, Jefferson Community and Technical College, KY, U.S.; **Rachel DeSanto**, Hillsborough Community College Dale Mabry Campus, FL, U.S.; **Nilüfer Ertürkmen**, Ege University, Turkey; **Sue Fine**, Ras Al Khaimah Women's College (HCT), U.A.E.; **Amina Al Hashami**, Nizwa College of Applied Sciences, Oman; **Stephan Johnson**, Nagoya Shoka Daigaku, Japan; **Sean Kim**, Avalon, South Korea; **Gregory King**, Chubu Daigaku, Japan; **Seran Küçük**, Maltepe University, Turkey; **Jonee De Leon**, VUS, Vietnam; **Carol Lowther**, Palomar College, CA, U.S.; **Erin Harris-MacLead**, St. Mary's University, NS, Canada; **Angela Nagy**, Maltepe University, Turkey; **Huynh Thi Ai Nguyen**, Vietnam; **Daniel L. Paller**, Kinjo Gakuin University, Japan; **Jangyo Parsons**, Kookmin University, South Korea; **Laila Al Qadhi**, Kuwait University, Kuwait; **Josh Rosenberger**, English Language Institute University of Montana, MT, U.S.; **Nancy Schoenfeld**, Kuwait University, Kuwait; **Jenay Seymour**, Hongik University, South Korea; **Moon-young Son**, South Korea; **Matthew Taylor**, Kinjo Gakuin Daigaku, Japan; **Burcu Tezcan-Unal**, Zayed University, U.A.E.; **Troy Tucker**, Edison State College-Lee Campus, FL, U.S.; **Kris Vicca**, Feng Chia University, Taichung; **Jisook Woo**, Incheon University, South Korea; **Dunya Yenidunya**, Ege University, Turkey

UNITED STATES **Marcarena Aguilar**, North Harris College, TX; **Rebecca Andrade**, California State University North Ridge, CA; **Lesley Andrews**, Boston University, MA; **Deborah Anholt**, Lewis and Clark College, OR; **Robert Anzelde**, Oakton Community College, IL; **Arlys Arnold**, University of Minnesota, MN; **Marcia Arthur**, Renton Technical College, WA; **Renee Ashmeade**, Passaic County Community College, NJ; **Anne Bachmann**, Clackamas Community College, OR; **Lida Baker**, UCLA, CA; **Ron Balsamo**, Santa Rosa Junior College, CA; **Lori Barkley**, Portland State University, OR; **Eileen Barlow**, SUNY Albany, NY; **Sue Bartch**, Cuyahoga Community College, OH; **Lora Bates**, Oakton High School, VA; **Barbara Batra**, Nassau County Community College, NY; **Nancy Baum**, University of Texas at Arlington, TX; **Rebecca Beck**, Irvine Valley College, CA; **Linda Berendsen**, Oakton Community College, IL; **Jennifer Binckes Lee**, Howard Community College, MD; **Grace Bishop**, Houston Community College, TX; **Jean W. Bodman**, Union County College, NJ; **Virginia Bouchard**, George Mason University, VA; **Kimberley Briesch Sumner**, University of Southern California, CA; **Kevin Brown**, University of California, Irvine, CA; **Laura Brown**, Glendale Community College, CA; **Britta Burton**, Mission College, CA; **Allison L. Callahan**, Harold Washington College, IL; **Gabriela Cambiasso**, Harold Washington College, IL; **Jackie Campbell**, Capistrano Unified School District, CA; **Adele C. Camus**, George Mason University, VA; **Laura Chason**, Savannah College, GA; **Kerry Linder Catana**, Language Studies International, NY; **An Cheng**, Oklahoma State University, OK; **Carole Collins**, North Hampton Community College, PA; **Betty R. Compton**, Intercultural Communications College, HI; **Pamela Couch**, Boston University, MA; **Fernanda Crowe**, Intrax International Institute, CA; **Vicki Curtis**, Santa Cruz, CA; **Margo Czinski**, Washtenaw Community College, MI; **David Dahnke**, Lone Star College, TX; **Gillian M. Dale**, CA; **L. Dalgish**, Concordia College, MN; **Christopher Davis**, John Jay College, NY; **Sherry Davis**, Irvine University, CA; **Natalia de Cuba**, Nassau County Community College, NY; **Sonia Delgadillo**, Sierra College, CA; **Esmeralda Diriye**, Cypress College & Cal Poly, CA; **Marta O. Dmytrenko-Ahrabian**, Wayne State University, MI; **Javier Dominguez**, Central High School, SC; **Jo Ellen Downey-Greer**, Lansing Community College, MI; **Jennifer Duclos**, Boston University, MA; **Yvonne Duncan**, City College of San Francisco, CA; **Paul Dydman**, USC Language Academy, CA; **Anna Eddy**, University of Michigan-Flint, MI; **Zohan El-Gamal**, Glendale Community College, CA; **Jennie Farnell**, University of Connecticut, CT; **Susan Fedors**, Howard Community College, MD; **Valerie Fiechter**, Mission College, CA; **Ashley Fifer**, Nassau County Community College, NY; **Matthew Florence**, Intrax International Institute, CA; **Kathleen Flynn**, Glendale College, CA; **Elizabeth Fonsea**, Nassau County Community College, NY; **Eve Fonseca**, St. Louis Community College, MO; **Elizabeth Foss**, Washtenaw Community College, MI; **Duff C. Galda**, Pima Community College, AZ; **Christiane Galvani**, Houston Community College, TX; **Gretchen Gerber**, Howard Community College, MD; **Ray Gonzalez**, Montgomery College, MD; **Janet Goodwin**, University of California, Los Angeles, CA; **Alyona Gorokhova**, Grossmont College, CA; **John Graney**, Santa Fe College, FL; **Kathleen Green**, Central High School, AZ; **Nancy Hamadou**, Pima Community College-West Campus, AZ; **Webb Hamilton**, De Anza College, San Jose City College, CA; **Janet Harclerode**, Santa Monica Community College, CA; **Sandra Hartmann**, Language and Culture Center, TX; **Kathy Haven**, Mission College, CA; **Roberta Hendrick**, Cuyahoga Community College, OH; **Ginny Heringer**, Pasadena City College, CA; **Adam Henricksen**, University of Maryland, MD; **Carolyn Ho**, Lone Star College-CyFair, TX; **Peter Hoffman**, LaGuardia Community College, NY; **Linda Holden**, College of Lake County, IL; **Jana Holt**, Lake Washington Technical College, WA; **Antonio Iccarino**, Boston University, MA; **Gail Ibele**, University of Wisconsin, WI; **Nina Ito**, American Language Institute, CSU Long Beach, CA; **Linda Jensen**, UCLA, CA; **Lisa Jurkowitz**, Pima Community College, CA; **Mandy Kama**, Georgetown University, Washington, DC; **Stephanie Kasuboski**, Cuyahoga Community College, OH; **Chigusa Katoku**, Mission College, CA; **Sandra Kawamura**, Sacramento City College, CA; **Gail Kellersberger**, University of Houston-Downtown, TX; **Jane Kelly**, Durham Technical Community College, NC; **Maryanne Kildare**, Nassau County Community College, NY; **Julie Park Kim**, George Mason University, VA; **Kindra Kinyon**, Los Angeles Trade-Technical College, CA; **Matt Kline**, El Camino College, CA; **Lisa Kovacs-Morgan**, University of California, San Diego, CA; **Claudia Kupiec**, DePaul University, IL; **Renee La Rue**, Lone Star College-Montgomery, TX; **Janet Langon**, Glendale College, CA; **Lawrence Lawson**, Palomar College, CA; **Rachele Lawton**, The Community College of Baltimore County, MD; **Alice Lee**, Richland College, TX; **Esther S. Lee**, CSUF & Mt. SAC, CA; **Cherie Lenz-Hackett**, University of Washington, WA; **Joy Leventhal**, Cuyahoga Community College, OH; **Alice Lin**, UCI Extension, CA; **Monica Lopez**, Cerritos College, CA; **Dustin Lovell**, FLS International Marymount College, CA; **Carol Lowther**, Palomar College, CA; **Candace Lynch-Thompson**, North Orange County Community College District, CA; **Thi Thi Ma**, City College of San Francisco, CA; **Steve Mac Isaac**, USC Long Academy, CA; **Denise Maduli-Williams**, City College of San Francisco, CA; **Eileen Mahoney**, Camelback High School, AZ; **Naomi Mardock**, MCC-Omaha, NE; **Brigitte Maronde**, Harold Washington College, IL; **Marilyn Marquis**, Laposita College CA; **Doris Martin**, Glendale Community College; Pasadena City College, CA; **Keith Maurice**, University of Texas at Arlington, TX; **Nancy Mayer**, University of Missouri-St. Louis, MO; **Aziah McNamara**, Kansas State University, KS; **Billie McQuillan**, Education Heights, MN; **Karen Merritt**, Glendale Union High School District, AZ; **Holly Milkowart**, Johnson County Community College, KS; **Eric Moyer**, Intrax International Institute, CA; **Gino Muzzatti**, Santa Rosa Junior College, CA; **Sandra Navarro**, Glendale Community College, CA; **Than Nyeinkhin**, ELAC, PCC, CA; **William Nedrow**, Triton College, IL; **Eric Nelson**, University of Minnesota, MN; **Than Nyeinkhin**, ELAC, PCC, CA; **Fernanda Ortiz**, Center for English as a Second Language at the University of Arizona, AZ; **Rhony Ory**, Ygnacio Valley High School, CA; **Paul Parent**, Montgomery College, MD; **Dr. Sumeeta Patnaik**, Marshall University, WV; **Oscar Pedroso**, Miami Dade College, FL; **Robin Persiani**, Sierra College, CA; **Patricia Prenz-Belkin**, Hostos Community College, NY; **Suzanne Powell**, University of Louisville, KY; **Jim Ranalli**, Iowa State University, IA; **Toni R. Randall**, Santa Monica College, CA; **Vidya Rangachari**, Mission College, CA; **Elizabeth Rasmussen**, Northern Virginia Community College, VA; **Lara Ravitch**, Truman College, IL;

Deborah Repasz, San Jacinto College, TX; **Marisa Recinos**, English Language Center, Brigham Young University, UT; **Andrey Reznikov**, Black Hills State University, SD; **Alison Rice**, Hunter College, NY; **Jennifer Robles**, Ventura Unified School District, CA; **Priscilla Rocha**, Clark County School District, NV; **Dzidra Rodins**, DePaul University, IL; **Maria Rodriguez**, Central High School, AZ; **Josh Rosenberger**, English Language Institute University of Montana, MT; **Alice Rosso**, Bucks County Community College, PA; **Rita Rozzi**, Xavier University, OH; **Maria Ruiz**, Victor Valley College, CA; **Kimberly Russell**, Clark College, WA; **Stacy Sabraw**, Michigan State University, MI; **Irene Sakk**, Northwestern University, IL; **Deborah Sandstrom**, University of Illinois at Chicago, IL; **Jenni Santamaria**, ABC Adult, CA; **Shaeley Santiago**, Ames High School, IA; **Peg Sarosy**, San Francisco State University, CA; **Alice Savage**, North Harris College, TX; **Donna Schaeffer**, University of Washington, WA; **Karen Marsh Schaeffer**, University of Utah, UT; **Carol Schinger**, Northern Virginia Community College, VA; **Robert Scott**, Kansas State University, KS; **Suell Scott**, Sheridan Technical Center, FL; **Shira Seaman**, Global English Academy, NY; **Richard Seltzer**, Glendale Community College, CA; **Harlan Sexton**, CUNY Queensborough Community College, NY; **Kathy Sherak**, San Francisco State University, CA; **German Silva**, Miami Dade College, FL; **Ray Smith**, Maryland English Institute, University of Maryland, MD; **Shira Smith**, NICE Program University of Hawaii, HI; **Tara Smith**, Felician College, NJ; **Monica Snow**, California State University, Fullerton, CA; **Elaine Soffer**, Nassau County Community College, NY; **Andrea Spector**, Santa Monica Community College, CA; **Jacqueline Sport**, LBWCC Luverne Center, AL; **Karen Stanely**, Central Piedmont Community College, NC; **Susan Stern**, Irvine Valley College, CA; **Ayse Stromsdorfer**, Soldan I.S.H.S., MO; **Yilin Sun**, South Seattle Community College, WA; **Thomas Swietlik**, Intrax International Institute, IL; **Nicholas Taggert**, University of Dayton, OH; **Judith Tanka**, UCLA Extension–American Language Center, CA; **Amy Taylor**, The University of Alabama Tuscaloosa, AL; **Andrea Taylor**, San Francisco State, CA; **Priscilla Taylor**, University of Southern California, CA; **Ilene Teixeira**, Fairfax County Public Schools, VA; **Shirl H. Terrell**, Collin College, TX; **Marya Teutsch-Dwyer**, St. Cloud State University, MN; **Stephen Thergesen**, ELS Language Centers, CO; **Christine Tierney**, Houston Community College, TX; **Arlene Turini**, North Moore High School, NC; **Cara Tuzzolino**, Nassau County Community College, NY; **Suzanne Van Der Valk**, Iowa State University, IA; **Nathan D. Vasarhely**, Ygnacio Valley High School, CA; **Naomi S. Verratti**, Howard Community College, MD; **Hollyahna Vettori**, Santa Rosa Junior College, CA; **Julie Vorholt**, Lewis & Clark College, OR; **Danielle Wagner**, FLS International Marymount College, CA; **Lynn Walker**, Coastline College, CA; **Laura Walsh**, City College of San Francisco, CA; **Andrew J. Watson**, The English Bakery; **Donald Weasenforth**, Collin College, TX; **Juliane Widner**, Sheepshead Bay High School, NY; **Lynne Wilkins**, Mills College, CA; **Pamela Williams**, Ventura College, CA; **Jeff Wilson**, Irvine Valley College, CA; **James Wilson**, Consomnes River College, CA; **Katie Windahl**, Cuyahoga Community College, OH; **Dolores "Lorrie" Winter**, California State University at Fullerton, CA; **Jody Yamamoto**, Kapiʻolani Community College, HI; **Ellen L. Yaniv**, Boston University, MA; **Norman Yoshida**, Lewis & Clark College, OR; **Joanna Zadra**, American River College, CA; **Florence Zysman**, Santiago Canyon College, CA;

CANADA Patricia Birch, Brandon University, MB; **Jolanta Caputa**, College of New Caledonia, BC; **Katherine Coburn**, UBC's ELI, BC; **Erin Harris-Macleod**, St. Mary's University, NS; **Tami Moffatt**, English Language Institute, BC; **Jim Papple**, Brock University, ON; **Robin Peace**, Confederation College, BC;

ASIA Rabiatu Abubakar, Eton Language Centre, Malaysia; **Wiwik Andreani**, Bina Nusantara University, Indonesia; **Frank Bailey**, Baiko Gakuin University, Japan; **Mike Baker**, Kosei Junior High School, Japan; **Leonard Barrow**, Kanto Junior College, Japan; **Herman Bartelen**, Japan; **Siren Betty**, Fooyin University, Kaohsiung; **Thomas E. Bieri**, Nagoya College, Japan; **Natalie Brezden**, Global English House, Japan; **MK Brooks**, Mukogawa Women's University, Japan; **Truong Ngoc Buu**, The Youth Language School, Vietnam; **Charles Cabell**, Toyo University, Japan; **Fred Carruth**, Matsumoto University, Japan; **Frances Causer**, Seijo University, Japan; **Jeffrey Chalk**, SNU, South Korea; **Deborah Chang**, Wenzao Ursuline College of Languages, Kaohsiung; **David Chatham**, Ritsumeikan University, Japan; **Andrew Chih Hong Chen**, National Sun Yat-sen University, Kaohsiung; **Christina Chen**, Yu-Tsai Bilingual Elementary School, Taipei; **Hui-chen Chen**, Shi-Lin High School of Commerce, Taipei; **Seungmoon Choe**, K2M Language Institute, South Korea; **Jason Jeffree Cole**, Coto College, Japan; **Le Minh Cong**, Vungtau Tourism Vocational College, Vietnam; **Todd Cooper**, Toyama National College of Technology, Japan; **Marie Cosgrove**, Daito Bunka

University, Japan; **Randall Cotten**, Gifu City Women's College, Japan; **Tony Cripps**, Ritsumeikan University, Japan; **Andy Cubalit**, CHS, Thailand; **Daniel Cussen**, Takushoku University, Japan; **Le Dan**, Ho Chi Minh City Electric Power College, Vietnam; **Simon Daykin**, Banghwa-dong Community Centre, South Korea; **Aimee Denham**, ILA, Vietnam; **Bryan Dickson**, David's English Center, Taipei; **Nathan Ducker**, Japan University, Japan; **Ian Duncan**, Simul International Corporate Training, Japan; **Nguyen Thi Kieu Dung**, Thang Long University, Vietnam; **Truong Quang Dung**, Tien Giang University, Vietnam; **Nguyen Thi Thuy Duong**, Vietnamese American Vocational Training College, Vietnam; **Wong Tuck Ee**, Raja Tun Azlan Science Secondary School, Malaysia; **Emilia Effendy**, International Islamic University Malaysia, Malaysia; **Bettizza Escueta**, KMUTT, Thailand; **Robert Eva**, Kaisei Girls High School, Japan; **Jim George**, Luna International Language School, Japan; **Jurgen Germeys**, Silk Road Language Center, South Korea; **Wong Ai Gnoh**, SMJK Chung Hwa Confucian, Malaysia; **Sarah Go**, Seoul Women's University, South Korea; **Peter Goosselink**, Hokkai High School, Japan; **Robert Gorden**, SNU, South Korea; **Wendy M. Gough**, St. Mary College/Nunoike Gaigo Senmon Gakko, Japan; **Tim Grose**, Sapporo Gakuin University, Japan; **Pham Thu Ha**, Le Van Tam Primary School, Vietnam; **Ann-Marie Hadzima**, Taipei; **Troy Hammond**, Tokyo Gakugei University International Secondary School, Japan; **Robiatul ʻAdawiah Binti Hamzah**, SMK Putrajaya Precinct 8(1), Malaysia; **Tran Thi Thuy Hang**, Ho Chi Minh City Banking University, Vietnam; **To Thi Hong Hanh**, CEFALT, Vietnam; **George Hays**, Tokyo Kokusai Daigaku, Japan; **Janis Hearn**, Hongik University, South Korea; **Chantel Hemmi**, Jochi Daigaku, Japan; **David Hindman**, Sejong University, South Korea; **Nahn Cam Hoa**, Ho Chi Minh City University of Technology, Vietnam; **Jana Holt**, Korea University, South Korea; **Jason Hollowell**, Nihon University, Japan; **F. N. (Zoe) Hsu**, National Tainan University, Yong Kang; **Kuei-ping Hsu**, National Tsing Hua University, Hsinchu City; **Wenhua Hsu**, I-Shou University, Kaohsiung; **Luu Nguyen Quoc Hung**, Cantho University, Vietnam; **Cecile Hwang**, Changwon National University, South Korea; **Ainol Haryati Ibrahim**, Universiti Malaysia Pahang, Malaysia; **Robert Jeens**, Yonsei University, South Korea; **Linda M. Joyce**, Kyushu Sangyo University, Japan; **Dr. Nisai Kaewsanchai**, English Square Kanchanaburi, Thailand; **Aniza Kamarulzaman**, Sabah Science Secondary School, Malaysia; **Ikuko Kashiwabara**, Osaka Electro-Communication University, Japan; **Gurmit Kaur**, INTI College, Malaysia; **Nick Keane**, Japan; **Ward Ketcheson**, Aomori University, Japan; **Nicholas Kemp**, Kyushu International University, Japan; **Montchatry Ketmuni**, Rajamangala University of Technology, Thailand; **Dinh Viet Khanh**, Vietnam; **Seonok Kim**, Kangsu Jongro Language School, South Korea; **Suyeon Kim**, Anyang University, South Korea; **Kelly P. Kimura**, Soka University, Japan; **Masakazu Kimura**, Katoh Gakuen Gyoshu High School, Japan; **Gregory King**, Chubu Daigaku, Japan; **Stan Kirk**, Konan University, Japan; **Donald Knight**, Nan Hua/Fu Li Junior High Schools, Hsinchu; **Kari J. Kostiainen**, Nagoya City University, Japan; **Pattri Kuanpulpol**, Silpakorn University, Thailand; **Ha Thi Lan**, Thai Binh Teacher Training College, Vietnam; **Eric Edwin Larson**, Miyazaki Prefectural Nursing University, Japan; **David Laurence**, Chubu Daigaku, Japan; **Richard S. Lavin**, Prefectural University of Kumamoto, Japan; **Shirley Leane**, Chugoku Junior College, Japan; **I-Hsiu Lee**, Yunlin; **Nari Lee**, Park Jung PLS, South Korea; **Tae Lee**, Yonsei University, South Korea; **Lys Yongsoon Lee**, Reading Town Geumcheon, South Korea; **Mallory Leece**, Sun Moon University, South Korea; **Dang Hong Lien**, Tan Lam Upper Secondary School, Vietnam; **Huang Li-Han**, Rebecca Education Institute, Taipei; **Sovannarith Lim**, Royal University of Phnom Penh, Cambodia; **Ginger Lin**, National Kaohsiung Hospitality College, Kaohsiung; **Noel Lineker**, New Zealand/Japan; **Tran Dang Khanh Linh**, Nha Trang Teachers' Training College, Vietnam; **Daphne Liu**, Buliton English School, Taipei; **S. F. Josephine Liu**, Tien-Mu Elementary School, Taipei ; **Caroline Luo**, Tunghai University, Taichung; **Jeng-Jia Luo**, Tunghai University, Taichung; **Laura MacGregor**, Gakushuin University, Japan; **Amir Madani**, Visuttharangsi School, Thailand; **Elena Maeda**, Sacred Heart Professional Training College, Japan; **Vu Thi Thanh Mai**, Hoang Gia Education Center, Vietnam; **Kimura Masakazu**, Kato Gakuen Gyoshu High School, Japan; **Susumu Matsuhashi**, Net Link English School, Japan; **James McCrostie**, Daito Bunka University, Japan; **Joel McKee**, Inha University, South Korea; **Colin McKenzie**, Wachirawit Primary School, Thailand; **Terumi Miyazoe**, Tokyo Denki Daigaku, Japan; **William K. Moore**, Hiroshima Kokusai Gakuin University, Japan; **Kevin Mueller**, Tokyo Kokusai Daigaku, Japan; **Hudson Murrell**, Baiko Gakuin University, Japan; **Frances Namba**, Senri International School of Kwansei Gakuin, Japan; **Keiichi Narita**, Niigata University, Japan; **Kim Chung Nguyen**, Ho Chi Minh University of

Industry, Vietnam; **Do Thi Thanh Nhan**, Hanoi University, Vietnam; **Dale Kazuo Nishi**, Aoyama English Conversation School, Japan; **Huynh Thi Ai Nguyen**, Vietnam; **Dongshin Oh**, YBM PLS, South Korea; **Keiko Okada**, Dokkyo Daigaku, Japan; **Louise Ohashi**, Shukutoku University, Japan; **Yongjun Park**, Sangji University, South Korea; **Donald Patnaude**, Ajarn Donald's English Language Services, Thailand; **Virginia Peng**, Ritsumeikan University, Japan; **Suangkanok Piboonthamnont**, Rajamangala University of Technology, Thailand; **Simon Pitcher**, Business English Teaching Services, Japan; **John C. Probert**, New Education Worldwide, Thailand; **Do Thi Hoa Quyen**, Ton Duc Thang University, Vietnam; **John P. Racine**, Dokkyo University, Japan; **Kevin Ramsden**, Kyoto University of Foreign Studies, Japan; **Luis Rappaport**, Cung Thieu Nha Ha Noi, Vietnam; **Lisa Reshad**, Konan Daigaku Hyogo, Japan; **Peter Riley**, Taisho University, Japan; **Thomas N. Robb**, Kyoto Sangyo University, Japan; **Rory Rosszell**, Meiji Daigaku, Japan; **Maria Feti Rosyani**, Universitas Kristen Indonesia, Indonesia; **Greg Rouault**, Konan University, Japan; **Chris Ruddenklau**, Kindai University, Japan; **Hans-Gustav Schwartz**, Thailand; **Mary-Jane Scott**, Soongsil University, South Korea; **Dara Sheahan**, Seoul National University, South Korea; **James Sherlock**, A.P.W. Angthong, Thailand; **Prof. Shieh**, Minghsin University of Science & Technology, Xinfeng; **Yuko Shimizu**, Ritsumeikan University, Japan; **Suzila Mohd Shukor**, Universiti Sains Malaysia, Malaysia; **Stephen E. Smith**, Mahidol University, Thailand; **Moon-young Son**, South Korea; **Seunghee Son**, Anyang University, South Korea; **Mi-young Song**, Kyungwon University, South Korea; **Lisa Sood**, VUS, BIS, Vietnam; **Jason Stewart**, Taejon International Language School, South Korea; **Brian A. Stokes**, Korea University, South Korea; **Mulder Su**, Shih-Chien University, Kaohsiung; **Yoomi Suh**, English Plus, South Korea; **Yun-Fang Sun**, Wenzao Ursuline College of Languages, Kaohsiung; **Richard Swingle**, Kansai Gaidai University, Japan; **Sanford Taborn**, Kinjo Gakuin Daigaku, Japan; **Mamoru Takahashi**, Akita Prefectural University, Japan; **Tran Hoang Tan**, School of International Training, Vietnam; **Takako Tanaka**, Doshisha University, Japan; **Jeffrey Taschner**, American University Alumni Language Center, Thailand; **Matthew Taylor**, Kinjo Gakuin Daigaku, Japan; **Michael Taylor**, International Pioneers School, Thailand; **Kampanart Thammaphati**, Wattana Wittaya Academy, Thailand; **Tran Duong The**, Sao Mai Language Center, Vietnam; **Tran Dinh Tho**, Duc Tri Secondary School, Vietnam; **Huynh Thi Anh Thu**, Nhatrang College of Culture Arts and Tourism, Vietnam; **Peter Timmins**, Peter's English School, Japan; **Fumie Togano**, Hosei Daini High School, Japan; **F. Sigmund Topor**, Keio University Language School, Japan; **Tu Trieu**, Rise VN, Vietnam; **Yen-Cheng Tseng**, Chang-Jung Christian University, Tainan; **Pei-Hsuan Tu**, National Cheng Kung University, Tainan City; **Hajime Uematsu**, Hirosaki University, Japan; **Rachel Um**, Mok-dong Oedae English School, South Korea; **David Underhill**, EEExpress, Japan; **Ben Underwood**, Kugenuma High School, Japan; **Siriluck Usaha**, Sripatum University, Thailand; **Tyas Budi Utami**, Indonesia; **Nguyen Thi Van**, Far East International School, Vietnam; **Stephan Van Eycken**, Kosei Gakuen Girls High School, Japan; **Zisa Velasquez**, Taihu International School/Semarang International School, China/Indonesia; **Jeffery Walter**, Sangji University, South Korea; **Bill White**, Kinki University, Japan; **Yohanes De Deo Widyastoko**, Xaverius Senior High School, Indonesia; **Dylan Williams**, SNU, South Korea; **Jisuk Woo**, Ichean University, South Korea; **Greg Chung-Hsien Wu**, Providence University, Taichung; **Xun Xiaoming**, BLCU, China; **Hui-Lien Yeh**, Chai Nan University of Pharmacy and Science, Tainan; **Sittiporn Yodnil**, Huachiew Chalermprakiet University, Thailand; **Shamshul Helmy Zambahari**, Universiti Teknologi Malaysia, Malaysia; **Ming-Yuli**, Chang Jung Christian University, Tainan; **Aimin Fadhlee bin Mahmud Zuhodi**, Kuala Terengganu Science School, Malaysia;

CONTENTS

What risks are good to take?

A Discuss these questions with your classmates.

1. What are some risks that people take? Why do they take them?

2. What kinds of risks are OK to take? What kinds are not? Why?

3. Look at the photo. What kind of a risk is this man taking? Would you ever take this kind of risk? Why or why not?

B Listen to *The Q Classroom* online. Then answer these questions.

1. What types of risks do the students mention?

2. Why is it good to take social risks? What are the risks of changing jobs?

 C Go to the Online Discussion Board to discuss the Unit Question with your classmates.

UNIT OBJECTIVE ▶▶▶▶ Listen to a talk and a report and gather information and ideas to give a short presentation on a risk you have taken.

D Look at the questionnaire. Check (✓) your answers. Then read the answers below to find out if you are a risk taker.

Are you a risk taker?

Have you ever:	Yes, I have.	No, but I might.	No, I never will.
① moved to a new country?	☐	☐	☐
② gone on vacation without a place to stay?	☐	☐	☐
③ bought something you couldn't afford?	☐	☐	☐
④ done something others might think crazy?	☐	☐	☐
⑤ slept outside without a tent?	☐	☐	☐
⑥ stayed up late the night before an exam?	☐	☐	☐
⑦ made a promise that might be difficult to keep?	☐	☐	☐
⑧ ridden on the back of a motorcycle?	☐	☐	☐

Rate your answers

If you answered mostly yes: You like to take many different kinds of risks. You may get a thrill by taking risks. Life is fast and exciting. Sometimes, the risk will be worth it, but you could get into trouble.

If you answered mostly no: You play it safe. You are uncomfortable with risks. Your idea of a good time is staying home and reading a book. The good thing is that you will avoid trouble. On the other hand, you may not be as successful as some risk takers.

If your answers were mostly in the middle column or included some of each: You are middle-of-the-road. You are willing to take some risks, but not too many. You're careful, but willing to put yourself in uncomfortable situations if it's worth it.

E Discuss the answers in a group. Do you agree with the description of you? Why or why not? Give examples.

When people take risks, they do it because they want one or more outcomes. An outcome is a result, or an effect, of taking a certain action. When listening to a speaker talking about risks and outcomes, you can list the risks and outcomes for an action separately in a chart.

Action: Moving to a new city

Risks

- far away from friends/family
- have to quit job
- no apartment

Desired Outcomes

- find a better job in field
- take classes at the university
- meet new people

Signposts to listen for:

One possible risk is . . .
This is risky because . . .
One danger of this is . . .
You risk . . .
It threatens . . .

I hope to . . .
She wants to . . .
We take the risk in order to . . .
. . . far outweighs any risk.

A. Read this excerpt from a presentation about a new hobby. Then answer the questions on page 104.

For the past several years, I have played soccer every Thursday night on a club team. This year, I decided to try something different. I wanted to learn how to kayak but the class was on Thursday nights. I was nervous. Signing up for the kayaking class was a little risky because I would lose my spot on the soccer team. Also, I know how to play soccer, and I might be bad at kayaking. But I wanted to try something new. I was a little bored with soccer. Kayaking is also great exercise, and it is a new skill. I use different muscles. Also, I am meeting new people. You can kayak with other people, or you can kayak by yourself, so it's more flexible.

Kayaking

1. What action does the speaker talk about? _____

2. What were some risks?

   _____

   _____

3. What outcomes did the speaker hope for?

   _____

   _____

B. With a partner, summarize the speaker's points on the chart below.

Action:	
Risks	**Outcome**

iQ ONLINE **C.** Go online for more practice separating risks and outcomes with a chart.

LISTENING

LISTENING 1 | Write Your Own Success Story

 **UNIT OBJECTIVE** ▶▶▶▶ You are going to listen to a book reviewer talk about different risks writers take to get published. As you listen to the talk, gather information and ideas about what risks are good to take.

PREVIEW THE LISTENING

A. **PREVIEW** What are two risks a writer might take in order to get his or her book published?

B. **VOCABULARY** Read aloud these words and phrases from Listening 1. Check (✓) the ones you know. Use a dictionary to define any new or unknown words. Then discuss with a partner how the words will relate to the unit.

audience *(n.)* 🔑	**income** *(n.)* 🔑
embarrass *(v.)* 🔑	**model** *(n.)* 🔑
expose *(v.)* 🔑	**promote** *(v.)* 🔑
financial *(adj.)* 🔑	**publish** *(v.)* 🔑
funds *(n.)* 🔑	**threaten** *(v.)* 🔑

🔑 Oxford 3000™ words

 C. Go online to listen and practice your pronunciation.

WORK WITH THE LISTENING

🔊 **A.** **LISTEN AND TAKE NOTES** Listen to the talk about publishing. Before you listen, look at the chart below. As you listen, add information to the chart.

Writer	Action	Outcome
John Grisham		
Christopher Paolini and parents		
Brunonia Barry		
Amanda Hocking		

B. Work with a partner. Complete the chart with information from activity A.

Self-publishing and marketing	
Risks	**Outcome**

C. Read the statements. Write *T* (true) or *F* (false). Write supporting information from the listening. Then correct each false statement to make it true.

	Supporting information in the listening
__T__ **1.** For a long time, publishing your own book was a risk to your reputation.	It was embarrassing.
____ **2.** Publishers typically pay authors a large advance and also pay to promote the book.	
____ **3.** It's not hard to promote your own book.	
____ **4.** Even when a person publishes his or her own book, a major publisher may decide to buy it later.	
____ **5.** Because e-books are inexpensive to produce, they can be made available to more people.	

D. Listen again. Write the missing details in the chart.

Writer	Type of book	First publisher	What the writer did (strategies)
John Grisham		very small publishing company	
	adventure novel		
		their own software company	
Amanda Hocking			

E. Based on the information in the listening, complete each sentence with the best phrase.

1. Writers who publish their own books today get ___ those in the past.
   a. less respect than
   b. the same amount of respect as
   c. more respect than

2. For successful self-publishers, publication of the book is probably ___.
   a. the final step in a long process
   b. the beginning of a new stage of the process
   c. fairly easy

3. The speaker probably thinks self-publishing is ___.
   a. a bad idea
   b. an excellent idea
   c. an idea writers should think about

F. Read the situations below. All three of these people have written books, but can't find a publisher. Which strategies used by other writers do you think they should try? Discuss with a partner. Explain your reasons.

1. Marisa Jackson just graduated from college. She has written three young adult novels set in a strange new world. She uses social media a lot.

2. Howard Hart is a middle-aged lawyer. His work keeps him very busy. He has a lot of money in savings. He wrote an exciting courtroom drama.

3. Elena Marx is a single parent with two children in college. She works as an accountant and part-time in a bookstore. She has written and illustrated three children's books.

G. **VOCABULARY** Use the new vocabulary from Listening 1. Read the paragraph. Then fill in the blanks with the correct words from the list.

audience *(n.)*	expose *(v.)*	funds *(n.)*	model *(n.)*	publish *(v.)*
embarrass *(v.)*	financial *(adj.)*	income *(n.)*	promote *(v.)*	threaten *(v.)*

Learning about Money the Hard Way

When I went to college, I didn't know anything about

_____ matters. I didn't have very much money.
⠀⠀⠀⠀⠀⠀1

I wasn't working, so I didn't have a regular _____.
⠀⠀⠀⠀⠀⠀⠀⠀⠀⠀⠀⠀⠀⠀⠀⠀⠀⠀⠀⠀⠀⠀⠀⠀⠀⠀⠀⠀⠀⠀2

I started to buy things online or that I saw on TV. If an ad came on to

_____ a new product, I just had to have it. That way I could
⠀⠀⠀⠀⠀3

buy whatever I wanted without paying right away. Soon, I had a $25,000

credit card bill. When my parents found the bill, they were very upset.

They offered to give me the _____ I needed to pay it. They
⠀⠀⠀⠀⠀⠀⠀⠀⠀⠀⠀⠀⠀⠀⠀⠀⠀⠀⠀⠀⠀4

didn't want to _____ me, but told me I needed to be more
⠀⠀⠀⠀⠀⠀⠀⠀⠀⠀⠀5

responsible. I finally repaid them, but it took a long time. Now I work for

a bank and give talks to college students about managing their money. I

try to _____ the problems they can have if they owe a lot of
⠀⠀⠀⠀⠀6

money when they are in school. I explain that what I did was not a good

_____ to follow. The students in the _____
⠀⠀⠀⠀7⠀⠀⠀⠀⠀⠀⠀⠀⠀⠀⠀⠀⠀⠀⠀⠀⠀⠀⠀⠀⠀⠀⠀⠀⠀8

are always interested in the topic. They usually don't know that owing

so much money can _____ their future happiness.
⠀⠀⠀⠀⠀⠀⠀⠀⠀⠀⠀⠀⠀⠀⠀9

We are going to _____ a book soon about money and
⠀⠀⠀⠀⠀⠀⠀⠀⠀⠀10

college students.

---

iQ ONLINE **H.** Go online for more practice with the vocabulary.

SAY WHAT YOU THINK

Discuss the questions in a group.

1. Why do you think these writers took the risks they did?

2. Do you have any dreams or goals that might require you to take risks? What are they? What are some of the risks you might have to take to achieve them?

3. What careers do you think involve a lot of risk? Why?

Listening Skill **Part 1 Identifying amounts; cardinal and ordinal numbers**

Identifying amounts

When listening to amounts of money, first listen for the amounts (*fifty, one hundred, two thousand, million, billion*). Then listen for the units or currency (*dollars, euros, pounds*). It is important to remember that the way you say and hear amounts of money is different from the way you write them or see them when reading. For example, you will read and write *$300*, but you will hear *three hundred dollars*.

Listen to these examples.

$500	$200,000
£1,000	£5,000,000
€10,000	€12,000,000,000

Listen to this excerpt from Listening 1 and pay attention to the amounts you hear. Notice that the $, £, or € sign is always written to show amounts of money, but it is not always spoken, especially after the first reference.

They risked their savings, spending $50,000 on the publication and publicity.
She sold the rights for $2 million.

Using amounts as adjectives

It was a **fifty-dollar** shirt.
The **three-hundred-pound** football player needed a larger uniform.
The **four-hundred-seat** stadium was too small for the crowd.
It's a **fifteen-minute** bus ride to my office.

When you write an amount as an adjective before a noun, use hyphens between each word of the adjective. Notice that it is not in the plural.

✓ A five-hundred-dollar TV.
✗ A five-hundred-dollars TV.

A. Listen to the sentences. Complete the sentences with the amounts you hear. Do not write the dollar sign ($). Write out the amounts in words. If the amount is an adjective, use hyphens.

1. Christopher Paolini sold the rights to his novels for

   _____ .

2. The cheapest tickets are _____ .

3. The _____ bag of sugar is _____ .

4. The _____ stadium was too small for the crowd.

5. That store sells _____ shoes.

6. We took a _____ survey online.

7. My suitcase weighs over _____ .

8. Maria found a _____ bill on the sidewalk.

B. Work with a partner. Take turns asking and answering questions about the sentences in Activity A.

A: How much did Paolini sell his book rights for?

B: He sold them for five hundred thousand dollars.

Listening Skill | **Part 2 Identifying amounts; cardinal and ordinal numbers**

Identifying cardinal and ordinal numbers

Some **ordinal** numbers sound very different from **cardinal** numbers (*first/one, second/two, third/three*). Most sound very similar except they end in a **–th** sound (*sixteen/sixteenth, thirty/thirtieth*).

Listen to these cardinal and ordinal numbers. Pay attention to the **–th** sound at the end of most ordinal numbers.

cardinal	ordinal	cardinal	ordinal
one	first	seven	seventh
two	second	twenty	twentieth
three	third	thirty-four	thirty-fourth
five	fifth	forty-six	forty-sixth

C. Listen to the sentences. Check (✓) the sentence you hear.

1. ☐ The seven tests can be taken this week.
   ☐ The seventh test can be taken this week.

2. ☐ The nine students left an hour ago.
   ☐ The ninth student left an hour ago.

3. ☐ I ate the fifteen cookies.
   ☐ I ate the fifteenth cookie.

4. ☐ Did you receive the six emails I sent you?
   ☐ Did you receive the sixth email I sent you?

5. ☐ Push the four buttons.
   ☐ Push the fourth button.

D. Listen again. Repeat the sentences. Then take turns saying and identifying the sentences from Activity C with a partner.

iQ ONLINE   **E.** Go online for more practice identifying amounts and cardinal and ordinal numbers.

LISTENING 2 | Science on the Edge

UNIT OBJECTIVE ▶▶▶▶   You are going to listen to a report on scientists with risky jobs. As you listen to the report, gather information and ideas about what risks are good to take.

PREVIEW THE LISTENING

A. PREVIEW Which fields of science do you think are risky?

☐ drug research   ☐ studying volcanoes

☐ laboratory research   ☐ underwater exploration

☐ meteorology (weather)   ☐ your idea: _____

B. VOCABULARY Read aloud these words and phrases from Listening 2. Check (✓) the ones you know. Use a dictionary to define any new or unknown words. Then discuss with a partner how the words will relate to the unit.

discover (v.) 🔑	investigate (v.) 🔑	mystery (n.) 🔑	prove (v.) 🔑	retire (v.) 🔑
invention (n.) 🔑	locate (v.) 🔑	previous (adj.) 🔑	reputation (n.) 🔑	solve (v.) 🔑

🔑 Oxford 3000™ words

C. Go online to listen and practice your pronunciation.

WORK WITH THE LISTENING

A. **LISTEN AND TAKE NOTES** Listen to the report. Take notes in the chart as you listen.

	Risks taken	Outcomes
Paul Flaherty		
Tina Neal		

B. Work with a partner. Answer the questions with information from the chart.

1. What risks do they both take?

2. What outcomes do both hope for?

C. Read the statements. Write *T* (true) or *F* (false). Then correct each false statement to make it true.

___ 1. Flaherty and Nepal work in the same scientific field.

_____

___ 2. Weather is one of the biggest risks they face.

_____

___ 3. Both scientists gather information to help predict natural disasters.

_____

___ 4. Unfortunately, there isn't much they can do to control or lower their risks.

_____

D. Listen again. Who is the detail about? Write *F* (Flaherty), *N* (Neal), or *B* (both) on the line.

___ 1. is a pilot

___ 2. flies a lot as part of the job

___ 3. makes maps of safe areas

___ 4. provided information on Hurricane Katrina

___ 5. lives in Alaska

___ 6. uses data to protect people

___ 7. works for National Oceanic and Atmospheric Administration

___ 8. works for the U.S. Geological Survey

E. Complete the Venn diagram with information about the two scientists.

Paul Flaherty   Both   Tina Neal

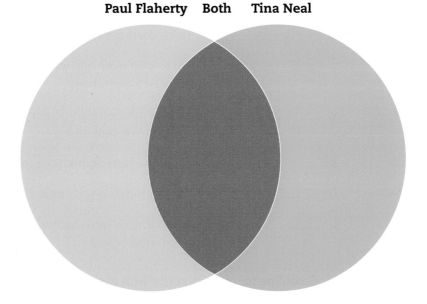

 F. Go online to listen to *The Blind Traveler* and check your comprehension.

Vocabulary Skill Review

In Unit 4, you learned how to use context clues to identify meaning. In Activity G, underline the clues in the sentences that help you identify the meaning of the words in bold.

G. VOCABULARY Use the new vocabulary from Listening 2. Read the sentences. Then write each bold word next to the correct definition.

1. Marie Curie was the first person to **discover** the elements polonium and radium.

2. My uncle's **invention** is a new machine that makes coffee and a doughnut at the same time.

3. For your next paper, I want you to **investigate** a topic that is interesting to you.

4. The police were unable to **locate** the stolen artifact.

5. Until recently, the nature of the planet Mars has been a **mystery**.

6. On my **previous** trip to Italy, I went to Venice, but I'm not going there this time.

7. Columbus was able to **prove** the earth was round.

8. That university has a very good **reputation**.

9. Dr. Arnesen enjoys his job so much, he says he never wants to **retire**.

10. Some of life's problems are too difficult for people to **solve** on their own.

a. _____ *(v.)* to find the exact position of someone or something

b. _____ *(v.)* to find a way of dealing with a problem or situation

c. _____ *(adj.)* coming or happening before or earlier

d. _____ *(v.)* to try to find out all the facts about something

e. _____ *(n.)* something that is made for the first time

f. _____ *(v.)* to stop working, usually because you have reached a certain age

g. _____ *(n.)* the opinion that people in general have about someone or something

h. _____ *(v.)* to use facts or evidence to show something is true

i. _____ *(n.)* a thing that you cannot understand or explain

j. _____ *(v.)* to find or learn something that no one knew or had found before

 H. Go online for more practice with the vocabulary.

 # SAY WHAT YOU THINK

A. Discuss the questions in a group.

1. Why do you think Flaherty and Neal are willing to take risks? Do you think they are different from most people? If so, how?

2. What other weather problems or natural disasters do we need to learn more about? What risks are involved in investigating them?

B. Before you watch the video, discuss the questions in a group.

1. What kinds of risks do scientists take today?

2. Why are people willing to try new and perhaps risky technologies?

 C. Go online to watch a video about a scientist collecting a sample from the Mount Nyiragongo volcano in the Democratic Republic of the Congo. Then check your comprehension.

deflect *(v.)* to prevent something from being directed toward you

lava *(n.)* hot liquid rock that comes out of a volcano

outrun *(v.)* to run faster than

retreat *(v.)* to move away or back

solidify *(v.)* to become solid

VIDEO VOCABULARY

D. Think about the unit video, Listening 1, and Listening 2 as you discuss the questions.

1. Why do people take risks in their careers? Is this a good thing? Why or why not?

2. Do you think people are more likely to take risks for professional reasons or in their personal life? Explain.

Vocabulary Skill   Word families

One way to increase your vocabulary is to understand **word families**. Word families consist of words that come from the same root and are related in form. They usually include several different parts of speech. For example, a noun may have an adjective and a verb form. The ending of the word often indicates the part of speech.

> **in·vent** /ɪnˈvɛnt/ *verb* [T] **1** to think of or make something for the first time: *Who invented the sewing machine?* ◆ *When was the camera invented?* **2** to say or describe something that is not true: *I realized that he had invented the whole story.* ▶ **in·ven·tor** /ɪnˈvɛntər/ *noun* [C]
>
> **in·ven·tion** /ɪnˈvɛnʃn/ *noun* **1** [C] a thing that has been made or designed by someone for the first time: *The microwave oven is a very useful invention.* **2** [U] the action or process of making or designing something for the first time: *Books had to be written by hand before the invention of printing.* **3** [C, U] telling a story or giving an excuse that is not true: *This story is apparently a complete invention.*
>
> **in·ven·tive** /ɪnˈvɛntɪv/ *adj.* having new and interesting ideas ▶ **in·ven·tive·ness** *noun* [U]

When you look up new words in the dictionary, look at the other words in the same word family. By doing this, you can add several new words to your vocabulary.

Another benefit of understanding word families is that when you see new words that look similar to words you already know, you can use your knowledge to figure out their meaning.

All dictionary entries are from the *Oxford American Dictionary for learners of English*
© Oxford University Press 2011.

Critical Thinking **Tip**

The chart in Activity A **categorizes** words by their part of speech. **Categorizing** is placing things into different groups. It can help you see similarities within groups and differences between groups.

A. Work with a partner. Complete the word family chart with any forms of the words you know. Use a dictionary to check your answers.

Verb	Noun	Adjective	Adverb
invent	inventor	inventive	inventively
		creative	
discover			
embarrass			
		financial	
locate			
prove		proven	
solve			

B. Complete each sentence with an appropriate word from Activity A. You may need to change the form.

1. Children are often _____ in the ways they play.

2. I can't _____ this math problem.

3. The scientist made an important new _____.

4. Independent TV producers _____ their programs in different ways: from credit cards to private investors to personal savings.

5. The _____ to the problem is at the back of the book.

6. Having too much credit card debt can lead to _____ disaster.

7. Scientists have never found real _____ that aliens exist.

8. We decided not to buy the house because of its _____. It was too close to the freeway.

9. I can't _____ he took my money, but I think he did.

10. I spilled coffee all over the table and myself at the fancy restaurant last night—it was so _____!

iQ ONLINE **C.** Go online for more practice with word families.

SPEAKING

At the end of this unit, you will give a short presentation on a risk you have taken. Be sure to clearly explain your reasons for taking that risk.

Grammar | Past perfect

Use the **past perfect** to show the relationship between two events or actions that happened in the past. Use the past perfect to describe the first event or action that happened. Use the **simple past** to describe the second event or action.

Past perfect *(1st event)*	Simple past *(2nd event)*
I **had driven** for five hours.	I **went** straight to bed without dinner.

Past perfect *(1st event)*	Simple past *(2nd event)*
The match **had** already **started**.	We **arrived** late.

Use the past perfect with past time clauses that begin with *when, before, by the time,* and *until.*

Past perfect *(1st event)*	Simple past *(2nd event)*
He **had been** at work for hours	<u>when</u> we **called** him.
Paul **had driven** for an hour	<u>before</u> he **noticed** he had a flat tire.
They **had** already **eaten** dinner	<u>by the time</u> I **got** home.
I **hadn't heard** anything about it	<u>until</u> I **read** the paper this morning.

Note: The past perfect is often used with the adverbs *already, yet, never, ever,* and *just.*

A. Read the pairs of sentences. Write 1 next to the sentence that happened first. Write 2 next to the sentence that happened second. Then write one sentence. Use the past time clause in parentheses.

1. The scientist retired. __1__
   He began research on a new area of interest. __2__

   (before) <u>The scientist had retired before he began research on a new area of interest.</u>

2. I didn't hear about Brunonia Barry. ____
   I read the article. ____

   (until) _____

3. It started to rain. _____
   We finished hiking. _____

   (before) _____

4. Mari picked up the phone. _____
   It stopped ringing. _____

   (by the time) _____

5. My sister told me. _____
   I didn't realize my sweater was on backwards. _____

   (until) _____

6. Nawaf left his house. _____
   His mother called. _____

   (when) _____

7. I drank the cup of coffee. _____
   I realized it wasn't mine. _____

   (before) _____

8. We arrived at the airport. _____
   Our plane departed. _____

   (by the time) _____

B. Complete the sentences with information that is true for you. Then take turns reading your sentences with a partner.

1. I _____ when I got home yesterday.

2. I _____ until I started taking this class.

3. I _____ by the time I graduated from high school.

4. I _____ by the year 2000.

5. I _____ before I _____ .

C. Go online for more practice using the past perfect.

D. Go online for the grammar expansion.

The contraction *'d* is frequently used instead of *had* in affirmative statements with the past perfect. Noticing *had* and the contraction *'d* can help you better understand the order of past events.

Listen to these examples. The speaker joins *'d* to words that follow beginning with vowel sounds and certain consonant sounds (*l*, *r*). Notice that *'d* is not stressed.

> I**'d** already finished the test when the teacher collected our papers.
> He**'d** eaten at that restaurant before.
> We**'d** often talked about getting married.
> You**'d** left when we got there.
> She**'d** written her email before she received mine.

Do not use a contraction with questions. Notice that *had* is not stressed in these questions.

> **Had** you heard from him by the time you left?
> **Had** everyone finished the test by 2:00?

The contraction with negatives is *hadn't*.

> I **hadn't** finished my phone call by the time the train arrived.
> They **hadn't** gone to the mall before they ate dinner.

A. Listen to the sentences. Check (✓) the sentence you hear.

1. ☐ He worked at a bookstore.
   ☐ He'd worked at a bookstore.

2. ☐ We left when it started raining.
   ☐ We'd left when it started raining.

3. ☐ They answered the questions.
   ☐ They'd answered the questions.

4. ☐ I've eaten my lunch.
   ☐ I'd eaten my lunch.

5. ☐ You've already taken the test.
   ☐ You'd already taken the test.

6. ☐ She didn't work there.
   ☐ She hadn't worked there.

7. ☐ It hasn't started to rain.
   ☐ It hadn't started to rain.

8. ☐ Has he found it?
   ☐ Had he found it?

9. ☐ Have you called Alex?
   ☐ Had you called Alex?

 B. Listen again. Repeat the sentences. Then take turns saying and identifying the sentences from Activity A with a partner.

 C. Go online for more practice with the contraction of *had*.

Speaking Skill | **Giving a short presentation**

When you give a short presentation in class or at work, start by introducing your topic clearly.

Here are some phrases you can use to introduce your topic.

> I want to talk about …
> My topic is …
> This presentation is on …
> I'm going to talk about …

During your presentation, it is important to use words and phrases that help your audience understand the order of events and the reasons for them.

Here are some words and phrases you can use to help your audience follow and understand your presentation.

Order of events	Purpose/reason
First,	so …
Second,	so that …
After that,	in order to …
Then,	The reason I took this risk was …
Before	
By the time	

A. Listen to this presentation. Complete the sentences with the words and phrases you hear.

Learning Japanese

_____ a time I took a risk and it

1

turned out well. I'd always wanted to learn to speak Japanese.

When I was in high school, I started to take classes in Japanese.

_____ I graduated from college, I had studied

2

the language for eight years, but I still couldn't speak it very well,

_____ I decided to go to Japan to study.

3

I didn't know anyone there. My grandmother had given me money the

year before, _____ I used that for the trip.

4

_____ I left, I'd done some research on language

5

schools. I stayed in Japan for three months and met some great people

there. My Japanese improved a lot. _____ I finally

6

returned to my country, I had become fluent.

Tip for Success

When listening, make sure you maintain eye contact. This encourages the speaker and shows that you are interested.

B. Check (✓) the risks you would take to learn English. Add some of your own ideas.

☐ join a club or sports team where people speak English
☐ take classes in other subjects with native English speakers
☐ move to a new city or country
☐ meet and talk to native speakers
☐ travel in English-speaking countries
☐ (your idea) _____
☐ (your idea) _____

C. Work with a partner. Take turns talking about the risks you checked in Activity B. Use words and phrases from the Speaking Skill box on page 120.

 D. Go online for more practice with giving a short presentation.

UNIT OBJECTIVE ▶▶▶ In this assignment, you are going to give a one-minute presentation on a risk you have taken. As you prepare your presentation, think about the Unit Question, "What risks are good to take?" Use information from Listening 1, Listening 2, the unit video, and your work in this unit to support your presentation. Refer to the Self-Assessment checklist on page 124 .

CONSIDER THE IDEAS

Listen to one man talk about a risk he took and the reasons why he took it. Take notes as you listen. Then discuss the questions with a partner.

The Pantheon in Rome

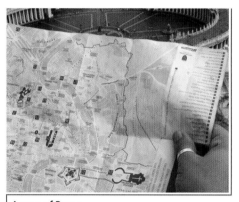
A map of Rome

What had his life been like before?

What did he risk by leaving?

Do you think it was a good risk to take? Why or why not?

What do you think happened when he arrived in Rome?

PREPARE AND SPEAK

A. **GATHER IDEAS** Think about the experience of the speaker in the Consider the Ideas activity above. Have you had a similar experience? What risks in your own life do you feel were good to take? Make a list.

_____

_____

_____

B. ORGANIZE IDEAS Choose one risk from your list in Activity A. Prepare to talk about it. Use the outline to help you organize your ideas.

The risk you took: _____

The reason why you took this risk:

_____

_____

_____

_____

Describe what happened:

_____

_____

_____

_____

_____

_____

_____

What did you learn or gain from this experience?

_____

_____

_____

_____

_____

_____

C. **SPEAK** Give a one-minute presentation to your group or class about a risk you have taken. Refer to the Self-Assessment checklist below before you begin.

1. Use an appropriate phrase to introduce your topic.

2. Use your notes from Activity B to help you, but do not read exactly what you wrote.

3. Try to talk continuously for the entire minute.

 Go online for your alternate Unit Assignment.

CHECK AND REFLECT

A. **CHECK** Think about the Unit Assignment as you complete the Self-Assessment checklist.

SELF-ASSESSMENT		
Yes	No	
☐	☐	I was able to speak easily about the topic.
☐	☐	My group or class understood me.
☐	☐	I used vocabulary from the unit.
☐	☐	I used the past perfect and simple past.
☐	☐	I used contractions of *had*.
☐	☐	I used phrases to introduce my topic, explain the order of events, and give reasons for events.

B. **REFLECT** Go to the Online Discussion Board to discuss these questions.

1. What is something new you learned in this unit?

2. Look back at the Unit Question—What risks are good to take? Is your answer different now than when you started this unit? If yes, how is it different? Why?

TRACK YOUR SUCCESS

Circle the words and phrases you have learned in this unit.

Nouns
audience 🔑
credit 🔑 AWL
debt 🔑
funds 🔑 AWL
income 🔑 AWL
invention 🔑
model 🔑
mystery 🔑
reputation 🔑

Verbs
discover 🔑
embarrass 🔑
expose 🔑 AWL
investigate 🔑 AWL
locate 🔑 AWL
promote 🔑 AWL
prove 🔑
publish 🔑 AWL
retire 🔑
solve 🔑
threaten 🔑

Adjectives
financial 🔑 AWL
previous 🔑 AWL

Phrases
I'm going to talk
   about …
I want to talk about …
in order to
My topic is …
This presentation is
   on …

🔑 Oxford 3000™ words
AWL   Academic Word List

Check (✓) the skills you learned. If you need more work on a skill, refer to the page(s) in parentheses.

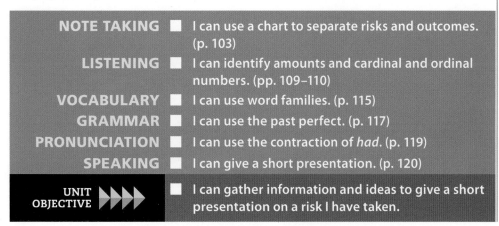

NOTE TAKING ◼	I can use a chart to separate risks and outcomes. (p. 103)
LISTENING ◼	I can identify amounts and cardinal and ordinal numbers. (pp. 109–110)
VOCABULARY ◼	I can use word families. (p. 115)
GRAMMAR ◼	I can use the past perfect. (p. 117)
PRONUNCIATION ◼	I can use the contraction of *had*. (p. 119)
SPEAKING ◼	I can give a short presentation. (p. 120)
UNIT OBJECTIVE ▶▶▶▶ ◼	I can gather information and ideas to give a short presentation on a risk I have taken.

UNIT QUESTION

Are we responsible for the world we live in?

A Discuss these questions with your classmates.

1. What does "to take responsibility" mean?

2. Do you think you are a responsible citizen?

3. Look at the photo. What are these people doing? Why?

B Listen to *The Q Classroom* online. Then answer these questions.

1. What three ways are mentioned as ways in which people can be responsible in their communities? Which of these things do you do? Which don't you do? Why not?

2. Felix says it is "not realistic to expect everyone to do those things" as they don't have time. Do you agree?

iQ ONLINE **C** Go online to watch a video about TOMS Shoes. Then check your comprehension.

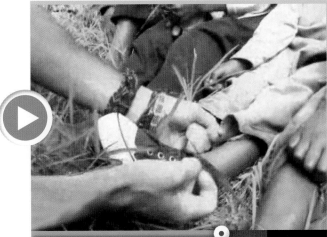

betterment *(n.)* the process of becoming or making someone or something better

stigma *(n.)* feelings of disapproval about certain illnesses or behavior

take it for granted *(phr.)* be so accustomed to something that you no longer think about its value

VIDEO VOCABULARY

  D Go to the Online Discussion Board to discuss the Unit Question with your classmates.

127

www.rolesandresponsibilities.survey   Search

ROLES *and* RESPONSIBILITIES

Who should be responsible for...

picking up litter: _____

reducing traffic accidents: _____

recycling used
bottles, paper, etc: _____

fighting crime: _____

making sure
children go to school: _____

taking care of the elderly: _____

Parents
Children
Individuals
Government
Volunteer groups
Charities
Other

F Work in a group. Discuss your ideas from Activity E. Give reasons for your answers. Then discuss how responsible you personally feel for each activity. Give examples of ways you take responsibility.

LISTENING 1 | Corporate Social Responsibility

UNIT OBJECTIVE ▶▶▶▶ You are going to listen to a lecture to a group of business students. As you listen to the lecture, gather information and ideas about responsibility in the world we live in.

PREVIEW THE LISTENING

A. PREVIEW The lecturer starts by defining "corporate social responsibility" and then discusses its importance in today's world. What do you think "corporate social responsibility" means? Discuss your ideas with a partner. Take notes on your discussion.

_____

_____

_____

_____

B. VOCABULARY Read aloud these words from Listening 1. Check (✓) the ones you know. Use a dictionary to define any new or unknown words. Then discuss with a partner how the words will relate to the unit.

benefit (n.) 🔑	**fine** (n.)
consumer (n.) 🔑	**ignore** (v.) 🔑
demand (v.) 🔑	**impact** (n.) 🔑
developed (adj.)	**pollute** (v.)
fair (adj.) 🔑	**profit** (n.) 🔑

🔑 Oxford 3000™ words

iQ ONLINE **C.** Go online to listen and practice your pronunciation.

WORK WITH THE LISTENING

A. **LISTEN AND TAKE NOTES** Listen to the lecture. As you listen, complete the notes.

> CSR is the belief that companies need to be responsible for the
>
> _____, social, and _____ impact of their actions.
>
> <u>Problems</u>
>
> - Child employment: No. of children working: _____ million
>
> (Reasons: They learn quickly and are _____.) dangerous conditions/no health care
>
> - Pollution of rivers/oceans
>
> <u>Pressure for change</u>
>
> Consumers: demanding that workers get a _____
>
> Workers: expect companies to protect their _____ /
>
> maybe provide _____, etc.
>
> _____: demanding companies reduce pollution
>
> <u>Who is responsible?</u>
>
> - international companies   - local _____
>
> - individual managers   - _____
>
> Important to realize that _____ and responsibility can go together.

B. Read the statements. Write *T* (true) or *F* (false) according to what the professor says.

____ 1. These days, more people are concerned about the impact companies have on the world we live in.

____ 2. The issue of corporate social responsibility affects only a small number of people.

____ 3. Companies in developed countries act more responsibly than those in developing countries.

____ 4. Pressure on companies to act more responsibly comes mainly from governments.

_____ 5. It's often difficult to decide who is responsible for the actions of a company.

_____ 6. It's not possible for companies to be socially responsible and to make a profit.

C. Read the sentences. Then listen again. Circle the answer that best completes each statement.

1. The professor says it's understandable that companies _____.
    a. want to make a profit
    b. find it difficult to be socially responsible

2. He adds that people in developed countries don't seem to be concerned about _____.
    a. the conditions of workers elsewhere
    b. the price they pay for products

3. He suggests that consumers are beginning to _____.
    a. demand that governments do more to help
    b. realize they can help change the situation

4. The professor thinks that it is not easy to decide who _____.
    a. is to blame for the problems
    b. should take more responsibility

5. He thinks that stopping child labor is something that _____.
    a. can be achieved soon
    b. we are all responsible for

D. What two ways does the professor say companies can be forced to behave more responsibly?

iQ ONLINE **E.** Go online to listen to *Buy One, Give One* and check your comprehension.

Vocabulary Skill Review

In Unit 4, you learned to identify meaning from context. Remember to read the whole sentence and consider the **context**. This can help you identify the correct word and meaning.

F. VOCABULARY Use the new vocabulary from Listening 1. Complete each sentence with the correct word from the box.

benefit (n.)	developed (adj.)	profit (n.)	fair (adj.)	impact (n.)
consumer (n.)	demand (v.)	fine (n.)	ignore (v.)	pollute (v.)

1. As a(n) _____, I always try to buy products from companies I know well.

2. Most people agree that companies should pay their workers a(n)

   _____ wage.

3. There are laws protecting workers. Most companies follow these laws,

   but some companies _____ them.

4. The company accepted responsibility for the accident and paid a large

   _____.

5. Some companies only care about money. Making a(n)

   _____ is more important to them than anything else.

6. Private health care is just one _____ that some companies

   give their workers.

7. Angry workers around the world are starting to _____

   more rights.

8. I think companies that _____ rivers with chemicals

   should be closed down.

9. People these days are more aware of the _____ of pollution

   on the environment.

10. _____ countries have a responsibility to help the

    global community.

 G. Go online for more practice with the vocabulary.

 # SAY WHAT YOU THINK

Discuss the questions in a group.

In discussion activities, always try to use words you have studied in the unit. This will help you learn the words and remember them in the future.

1. How important is it for companies to be socially responsible? What are the benefits?

2. Who do you think is more responsible for the actions of a company: the company itself or the individual decision-makers?

You can learn a lot about **a speaker's attitude** by noticing the way he talks. Someone who speaks slowly or sometimes hesitates before speaking might be nervous. Someone who raises her voice could be angry. Someone who is bored or uninterested might speak in a low voice with level intonation.

Listen to this excerpt from the lecture. Notice that the professor raises his voice. This indicates he feels passionately about the topic and is perhaps a little angry.

> We are all happy to buy our clothes more cheaply, but do we stop to think where they were made, and who made them?

Listen to this conversation. Notice that Speaker A speaks in a low voice with level intonation, expressing a lack of interest. Speaker B speaks slowly and hesitates. This shows he is nervous.

> **A:** It's the neighbor again. What does he want this time?
> **B:** Excuse me. Would you mind turning down the TV, please?
> **A:** Yeah, sure.

A. Listen to these sentences. Match each sentence with the speaker's attitude.

_____ 1. Did you know that this is a nonsmoking area?   a. uninterested

_____ 2. I don't know why Simon's always late for work.   b. angry

_____ 3. Yeah. That garbage has been there for a week.   c. nervous

B. Listen to each conversation. Check (✓) the word that describes how the woman feels.

1. ☐ uninterested   ☐ angry   ☐ nervous
2. ☐ uninterested   ☐ angry   ☐ nervous
3. ☐ uninterested   ☐ angry   ☐ nervous

C. Work with a partner. Take turns reading the sentences. Practice sounding angry, uninterested, or nervous. Your partner will try to identify how you feel.

1. Someone's left the front door open again.

2. I think there's something wrong with the engine.

3. Muna hasn't finished the report yet.

 D. Go online for more practice with inferring a speaker's attitude.

LISTENING 2 | Personal Responsibility

You are going to listen to an excerpt from a college seminar. As you listen to the excerpt, gather information and ideas about responsibility in the world we live in.

PREVIEW THE LISTENING

A. **PREVIEW** The students are discussing the issue of personal responsibility. Before you listen, think about the things you are responsible for in your daily life. Note your ideas, and then share them with the class.

B. **VOCABULARY** Read aloud these words from Listening 2. Check (✓) the ones you know. Use a dictionary to define any new or unknown words. Then discuss with a partner how the words will relate to the unit.

appropriate *(adj.)* 🔑	influence *(v.)* 🔑
check up on *(phr. v.)*	lie *(v.)* 🔑
guilty *(adj.)* 🔑	obligation *(n.)*
help out *(phr. v.)*	sensible *(adj.)* 🔑
in charge of *(phr.)*	trust *(v.)* 🔑

🔑 Oxford 3000™ words

 C. Go online to listen and practice your pronunciation.

WORK WITH THE LISTENING

 A. **LISTEN AND TAKE NOTES** Listen to the first part of a seminar on personal responsibility. Note the examples each student gives of ways in which they take individual responsibility at home.

Name	Notes
Naomi	
Michael	
Nina	
Mark	

B. Circle the answer that best completes each statement.

1. (All / Some) of the students feel it is important to help out at home.

2. Naomi's parents (help with / don't care about) recycling.

3. Michael helps out around the house (every day / only on Saturdays).

4. Nina usually (does all the cooking / helps in the evenings).

5. Mark takes care of his (little sister / pets).

C. Listen to the rest of the seminar. Circle the answer that best completes each statement.

1. _____ of the students say their parents always want to know where they are.
   a. All   b. Many   c. None

2. The students seem to be _____ that their parents check up on them.
   a. pleased   b. annoyed   c. proud

3. The students feel their parents don't _____ them enough.
   a. trust   b. listen to   c. support

4. According to the professor, the amount of responsibility parents give their children might depend on their _____.
   a. behavior   b. attitude   c. age

5. The students do not _____ at what age children are responsible.
   a. know   b. agree   c. understand

D. Complete the sentences.

1. Mark says his parents _____ him a lot when he is out.

2. Neil once _____ to his parents, but regretted it later.

3. Naomi thinks that anyone from the age of _____ is responsible for his or her actions.

4. According to Mark, teenagers need to be protected from the wrong _____.

5. Michael says it is possible for young children to learn to _____ other people.

E. What two reasons does Neil give to explain why his parents don't like him playing video games? Does he think his parents are right to be worried? What's your opinion?

F. VOCABULARY Use the new vocabulary from Listening 2. Read the sentences. Then write each bold word or phrase next to the correct definition.

1. My mother told me it's not **appropriate** to wear torn jeans to the event.

2. Amy's parents worry, so they always **check up on** her.

3. Sometimes I feel **guilty** when I don't tell my parents where I'm going.

4. My parents are always busy, so I'm glad to **help out** around the house.

5. Who is **in charge of** health and safety in your school?

6. You shouldn't let other people **influence** you all the time. You need to make your own decisions.

7. Do you agree it's wrong to **lie**, even if the truth can hurt?

8. A teacher's main **obligation** is to help students learn.

9. It's not very **sensible** to run across a busy road.

10. It's important to have good friends you can **trust**.

a. _____ *(phr. v.)* to make sure someone is behaving well

b. _____ *(v.)* to believe someone is honest and reliable

c. _____ *(adj.)* responsible for doing something wrong

d. _____ *(adj.)* showing the ability to act in a reasonable way

e. _____ *(v.)* to have an effect on

f. _____ *(n.)* something that you must do because it is your duty or because you promised to do it

g. _____ *(v.)* to say something that you know is not true

h. _____ *(phr.)* responsible for something

i. _____ *(phr. v.)* to assist by doing useful jobs

j. _____ *(adj.)* suitable or right for a particular situation, person, or use

 G. Go online for more practice with the vocabulary.

SAY WHAT YOU THINK

A. Discuss the questions in a group.

1. How much responsibility does your family give you? Are you content with this much responsibility?

2. At what age do you think someone becomes responsible for his or her actions (for example, behaving well in public, doing chores, or handling money)? Explain.

B. Think about the unit video, Listening 1, and Listening 2 as you discuss the questions.

1. What should companies do to protect the environment? In what ways should individuals be responsible for the environment? Who has more responsibility?

2. In what ways do you take responsibility for the world you live in? Give examples.

Vocabulary Skill | Using the dictionary

Finding the correct meaning

Words listed in a dictionary often have several meanings. To choose the correct meaning, first identify the part of speech (*noun, verb, adjective*, etc.). Then read all the definitions and example sentences. Finally, choose the meaning that best matches the context.

For example, read this conversation.

> **Nour:** Look, May. I found this gold ring in the park. It fits me perfectly!
>
> **May:** You're not going to keep it, are you? That's wrong! Turn it in to the police.

W*rong* can be a verb, noun, adjective, or adverb. Here, *wrong* is an adjective. W*rong (adj.)* in this dictionary has four different meanings. By considering the context and comparing examples, you will find that the most appropriate definition is Number 4—"not good or right."

> **wrong¹** /rɔŋ/ *adj.* **1** not true or not correct; not right: *the wrong answer* ◆ *You have the wrong number* (= on the telephone). ◆ *I think you're wrong about that.* **ANT** **right** **2** not the best; not suitable: *That's the wrong way to hold the bat.* ◆ *I think she married the wrong man.* **ANT** **right** **3** (not before a noun) **wrong (with sb/sth)** causing problems or difficulties; not as it should be: *You look upset. Is something wrong?* ◆ *What's wrong with the car this time?* ◆ *She has something wrong with her leg.* **4 wrong (to do sth)** bad or against the law; not good or right: *It's wrong to tell lies.* ◆ *The man said that he had done nothing wrong.*

All dictionary entries are from the *Oxford American Dictionary for learners of English* © Oxford University Press 2011.

A. Read the sentences. Use a dictionary. Follow the steps in the Vocabulary Skill box on page 137 to identify the correct meaning of each bold word. Then write the definition.

1. People living in a **just** society should respect the law.

   (adjective) fair and right, reasonable

2. Complaints against dishonest politicians have reached a **peak** in the last few years.

   _____

3. If it doesn't stop raining soon, I think we should **abandon** the idea of going for a walk.

   _____

4. I don't have **outstanding** bills. I paid them all on Wednesday.

   _____

5. People in positions of authority shouldn't **abuse** their power.

   _____

6. Terri lives a very **moral** life. She's a good example for her children.

   _____

7. Companies that continue to pollute the environment **risk** getting heavy fines.

   _____

8. In any relationship, it's important to be **open** and supportive.

   _____

B. Choose five words from Activity A and write your own sentences in your notebook. Then compare your sentences with a partner.

iQ ONLINE **C.** Go online for more practice using the dictionary.

SPEAKING

UNIT OBJECTIVE ▶▶▶▶ At the end of this unit, you will take part in a group discussion. Make sure to take turns leading the group discussion.

Grammar   Gerunds and infinitives as the objects of verbs

A **gerund** is **the base form of the verb + -ing**. Gerunds can be used as the objects of certain verbs, e.g., *admit, avoid, discuss, dislike, enjoy, finish, miss, quit*.

> Nigel enjoys **doing** the chores.
> After she left home, Emily missed **seeing** her family.

An **infinitive** is ***to* + the base form of the verb**. Infinitives can also be used as the objects of certain verbs, e.g., *agree, choose, decide, hope, learn, need, plan, want*.

> Managers decided **to ignore** safety concerns.
> The company plans **to reduce** pollution by 10 percent over the next year.

Some verbs can be followed by either a gerund or an infinitive, with no difference in meaning, e.g., *begin, hate, like, love, prefer*.

> Workers at the factory began **demanding** better conditions and more pay.
> Workers at the factory began **to demand** better conditions and more pay.

A. Circle the correct verb forms to complete the conversation. If both the infinitive and the gerund are possible, circle both answers. Then practice the conversation with a partner.

Vicky: Hey, Janice. Did you hear the news? My boss agreed (<u>giving / to give</u>)
₁ me a promotion last month.

Janice: That's great! Well done, Vicky. So, now your life is all about work, work, work, right?

Vicky: Yeah, but I hope (<u>to become / becoming</u>) vice president next year. Are
₂ you sorry you left the company?

Janice: Of course not! I love (<u>staying / to stay</u>) at home with my daughter. I don't
₃ miss (<u>working / to work</u>) in an office at all.
₄

Vicky: Hmm. I can't believe you chose (<u>quitting / to quit</u>). I thought you

wanted (<u>to stay / staying</u>) at the company for at least five more years.

Janice: Well, I did! But when I became a mother my priorities changed, I guess.

I felt I needed (<u>to spend / spending</u>) time at home with my daughter. My

husband and I have saved a lot of money, so I don't need (<u>having / to have</u>)

a job right now.

B. Write answers to the questions. Then discuss your answers with
a partner.

1. Do you think a mother should quit working to look after her child?

   _____

2. At what age would you want to become a parent?

   _____

3. Do you think parents miss looking after their children after they leave
   home?

   _____

4. How responsible do children need to feel for their parents when they are
   elderly?

   _____

C. Go online for more practice with gerunds and infinitives as the objects
of verbs.

D. Go online for the grammar expansion.

Speakers usually put more **stress** on the important words in a sentence, such as *nouns*, *verbs*, *adjectives*, and *adverbs*. These words are usually louder and clearer than other words in the sentence. Listening for stressed words can help you hear and understand the most important information.

Listen to this extract from Listening 1. Notice how the speaker stresses the important words.

> **We** are all **happy** to **buy** our **clothes** more **cheaply**, but do we **stop** to **think where** they were **made**, and **who made** them? Do you **know** who **made** your **jeans**, your **shirt**, or your **running shoes**?

A. Listen to more sentences from Listening 1. Underline the stressed words.

1. Corporate social responsibility is becoming a big issue these days.

2. Of course, companies want to make money. There's nothing wrong with that.

3. What is the cost to us, the planet, and the society we live in?

4. Imagine a company is polluting the environment. Who is responsible?

5. More and more consumers are demanding that companies pay their workers a fair wage.

B. Listen again. Repeat the sentences. Practice stressing the important words.

C. Read the extract below. Underline the important words that should be stressed. Then listen and check your answers.

> As consumers demand higher standards, more companies are trying to improve the lives of their workers and the society they live in. These companies show that profit, and social responsibility, can go together.

D. Listen again. Then read the extract aloud. Practice stressing the words you underlined in Activity C.

 E. Go online for more practice with word stress.

When discussing a topic in a group, it is important to choose one person to **lead the discussion**. The role of the leader is to guide the flow of the discussion. The leader

- starts the discussion
- gets comments from the members of the group
- keeps the discussion on topic
- ends the discussion

Here are some phrases you can use when you are leading a discussion.

Starting the discussion

The topic I'd like to discuss today is …
Today, we're going to discuss …
Our topic today is …

Getting comments from different people

What do you think, Massoud?
Kelly, what's your opinion?
Do you have anything to add, Charlene?

Keeping on topic

I think we need to return to the topic. What is your view on …?
Sorry, but can we keep to the topic?
Let's get back on topic.

Ending the discussion

That's all we have time for today.
To sum up, then, (summarize the main points)

A. Listen to this excerpt from a discussion on recycling. Complete the discussion with the phrases you hear. Then practice the discussion in a group of four.

Leader: OK, so today _____ recycling, and exactly

1

who should be responsible. Brad, _____?

2

Brad: Well, I think that basically as individuals we can't change much. It's the government that has to take action.

Leader: I see. _____, Seline?

3

Seline: I don't agree. We all need to do what we can. I mean, just one person can't do much … but everyone in the world acting together can change a lot! It's the same with raising money for charity. When everyone gives a little money, you can raise millions!

Brad: Yes. My brother ran a marathon for charity last year and …

Leader: Sorry, but _____? Susan,

4

_____?

5

Susan: Well, I probably agree with Brad. Recycling is such a big problem—you need the government to act, really.

Leader: OK, so _____, Susan and Brad feel the

6

government should take responsibility, while Seline thinks individuals should lead the way.

B. Work with a partner. Continue the discussion from Activity A, using your own ideas.

C. Go online for more practice leading a group discussion.

Building an outline is an effective way to take notes on a discussion. An outline is useful if you need to take comprehensive notes, as it will help you to make sure you cover all the main points. It will also show you how the different points relate to each other, as well as allow you to record examples and opinions in a systematic way.

To organize your notes in outline form, list the main points and then use indentation to record supporting points, opinions, and examples.

A. Study this outline from the discussion on recycling between Brad, Susan, and Seline. Notice how the main points and the details of their discussion are noted, along with their supporting ideas.

Topic *Who is responsible for recycling?*

(main point) • *The government should be responsible*

        (opinion) individuals can't change a lot

        (opinion) it's a big problem so the government should act

(main point) • *Individuals should take responsibility*

        (opinion) people must act together

        (supporting idea) raising money for charity – a little money from a lot of people = $ $ $

B. With a partner, think back to your discussion on recycling in Activity B on page 143. Add any additional opinions and supporting details or examples to the outline above.

C. Listen again to Listening 2. Complete this outline on the discussion.

(Topic)   *Individual responsibility*

(main point)   • *Children should help out at home*

(example) *take out* _____

(example) *sort recycling*

(opinion) *recycling is* _____

(example) *do dishes*

(example) *wash* _____

(example) *look after* _____

(example) *take care of pets*

(main point)   • *Parents should be responsible for their children*

(example) *know where their children are*

(example) _____ *them when they go out*

(opinion) *parents should* _____ *their children*

(main point)   • *Children should not lie to their parents*

(example) *should be truthful about what they are doing*

(supporting idea) *feel* _____ *if lie*

(main point)   • *Individual responsibility depends on age*

(opinion) *should know right from wrong at 16*

(opinion) *only responsible at 20*

(supporting idea) *at 16 can be easily* _____

(opinion) *responsible from 5 or 6*

(supporting idea) *possible to behave well/* _____ *others*

D. Go online for more practice building an outline to take notes on a discussion.

In this assignment, you are going to take part in a group discussion. As you prepare for the group discussion, think about the Unit Question, "Are we responsible for the world we live in?" Use information from Listening 1, Listening 2, the unit video, and your work in this unit to support your discussion. Refer to the Self-Assessment checklist on page 148.

CONSIDER THE IDEAS

Work in a group. Make a list of issues that affect your world (for example, pollution, crime, use of the Internet, etc.). Write your responsibilities concerning these issues below.

_____

_____

_____

_____

_____

_____

PREPARE AND SPEAK

A. GATHER IDEAS Read the statements. Check (✓) the ones you agree with.

☐ Individuals, not governments, are responsible for the society we live in.

☐ The content and use of the Internet need to be controlled.

☐ Global warming is something that only governments can fight effectively.

☐ Responsibility to your family is more important than anything else.

☐ It is OK for parents to spy on their children.

☐ Stealing is always wrong.

☐ We should all give money to support charities.

This activity asks you to **support your ideas**. When you support your ideas, you give reasons, examples, or details that help you prove your point. This helps you see strengths and weaknesses in your thinking.

B. **ORGANIZE IDEAS** Choose two statements from Activity A that you agree with and one that you disagree with. Complete the outline to help you prepare to give your opinion.

Agree

Statement: _____

Reasons: _____

_____

_____

Agree

Statement: _____

Reasons: _____

_____

_____

Disagree

Statement: _____

Reasons: _____

_____

_____

C. **SPEAK** Have a group discussion about whether or not we are responsible for the world we live in. Refer to the Self-Assessment checklist on page 148 before you begin.

1. Choose a leader for your discussion. The leader can begin the discussion by asking about your responses to the statements in Activity A.

2. When an issue you have written about in Activity B comes up for discussion, give your opinion and explain your reasons.

3. You can refer to your notes, but do not read exactly what you wrote.

4. Give each student a turn as group leader.

 Go online for your alternate Unit Assignment.

CHECK AND REFLECT

A. CHECK **Think about the Unit Assignment as you complete the Self-Assessment checklist.**

SELF-ASSESSMENT		
Yes	No	
☐	☐	I was able to speak easily about the topic.
☐	☐	My group understood me.
☐	☐	I used vocabulary from the unit.
☐	☐	I put stress on important words as I spoke.
☐	☐	I led a group discussion.
☐	☐	I used an outline to take notes on the discussion.

B. REFLECT **Go to the Online Discussion Board to discuss these questions.**

1. What is something new you learned in this unit?

2. Look back at the Unit Question—Are we responsible for the world we live in? Is your answer different now than when you started this unit? If yes, how is it different? Why?

TRACK YOUR SUCCESS

Circle the words and phrases you have learned in this unit.

Nouns
benefit 🔑 AWL
consumer 🔑 AWL
fine
impact 🔑 AWL
obligation
peak 🔑
profit 🔑

Verbs
abandon 🔑 AWL
abuse 🔑
demand 🔑
ignore 🔑 AWL
influence 🔑
lie 🔑
pollute
risk 🔑
trust 🔑

Adjectives
appropriate 🔑 AWL
developed
fair 🔑
guilty 🔑
just
moral 🔑
open 🔑
outstanding 🔑
sensible 🔑
wrong 🔑

Phrasal Verbs
check up on
help out

Phrases
Do you have anything to add?
in charge of
I think we need to return to the topic.
Let's get back on topic.
Our topic today is …
Sorry, but can we keep to the topic?
That's all we have time for today.
The topic I'd like to discuss today is …
To sum up, then,
Today, we're going to discuss …
What do you think?

🔑 Oxford 3000™ words
AWL Academic Word List

Check (✓) the skills you learned. If you need more work on a skill, refer to the page(s) in parentheses.

LISTENING ■	I can infer a speaker's attitude. (p. 133)
VOCABULARY ■	I can use a dictionary to find the correct meanings of words. (p. 137)
GRAMMAR ■	I can use gerunds and infinitives as the objects of verbs. (p. 139)
PRONUNCIATION ■	I can put stress on important words. (p. 141)
SPEAKING ■	I can lead a group discussion. (p. 142)
NOTE TAKING ■	I can build an outline to take notes on a discussion. (p. 144)

 **UNIT OBJECTIVE** ■ I can gather information and ideas to state and explain my opinions about our responsibility for issues impacting our world.

Can money buy happiness?

A Discuss these questions with your classmates.

1. How much money do you think people really need in order to be happy? Explain.

2. Do you think more money would make you happier? Why or why not?

3. Look at the photo. Would you be happier if you could buy a home like this? Why or why not?

B Listen to *The Q Classroom* online. Then answer these questions.

1. What things did the students mention they would do if they had more money?

2. According to Felix, what is something money can't buy?

 C Go to the Online Discussion Board to discuss the Unit Question with your classmates.

UNIT
OBJECTIVE ▶▶▶▶ Listen to a presentation and an interview and gather information and ideas to participate in a group discussion evaluating the influence money has on happiness.

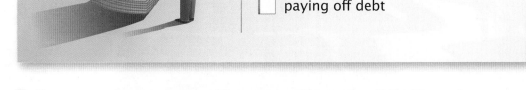

paying off debt

E Now compare your answers with a partner. Discuss the similarities and differences in your choices.

F Write the three things that make you the happiest. Then compare this list with the three things you chose in the questionnaire in Activity D. With your partner, discuss which list of things makes you happier and why.

_____

_____

_____

LISTENING 1 | Sudden Wealth

You are going to listen to a presentation on how people can change when they suddenly become rich. As you listen to the presentation, gather information and ideas about money and happiness.

PREVIEW THE LISTENING

A. **PREVIEW** Which topics do you think will be presented? Check (✓) your ideas.

☐ how sudden wealth makes people happy

☐ how sudden wealth causes problems

☐ the advantages and disadvantages of sudden wealth

Tip for Success

A question and answer early in a talk often indicates the speaker's main topic.

B. **VOCABULARY** Read aloud these words from Listening 1. Check (✓) the ones you know. Use a dictionary to define any new or unknown words. Then discuss with a partner how the words will relate to the unit.

acquire (v.) 🔑	destructive (adj.)	immediate (adj.) 🔑
circumstances (n.) 🔑	dramatic (adj.) 🔑	pleasure (n.) 🔑
complicated (adj.) 🔑	get used to (phr.)	wear off (phr. v.)

🔑 Oxford 3000™ words

iQ ONLINE **C.** Go online to listen and practice your pronunciation.

WORK WITH THE LISTENING

A. **LISTEN AND TAKE NOTES** Listen to the presentation about sudden wealth. Take notes in the chart as you listen.

Sudden Wealth	
Positive effects	**Negative effects**

B. Read the statements. Write *T* (true) or *F* (false). Then correct each false statement to make it true. Explain your answer with information from the listening.

	Supporting information in the listening
_F_ 1. Getting rich suddenly often ~~reduces~~ stress. causes	*People who acquire a sudden fortune . . . experience a lot of stress.*
____ 2. At first, acquiring a lot of money has a positive effect on our brains.	
____ 3. For most people, acquiring sudden wealth increases happiness.	
____ 4. Sudden wealth can cause many different problems.	
____ 5. People can feel more alone after they become suddenly wealthy.	

C. Listen again. Write two examples for each main point. Compare your ideas with a partner.

Effect on our brains

1. _____

2. _____

Effect on relationships

1. _____

2. _____

Effect on emotions

1. _____

2. _____

D. Read each situation. Based on the information in the listening, choose the best word or phrase to complete each sentence.

1. Mark got a great deal of money from his grandfather, but they didn't get along. Mark probably feels ____ .
   a. happy
   b. sad
   c. guilty

2. Elena received a very large bonus from her job. She bought a new car. After a month, she ____ .
   a. bought a new house
   b. opened a savings account
   c. gave the money away

3. Karen receives millions of dollars. She buys a house in an expensive town. After six months, she ____ .
   a. has all new friends
   b. misses her old friends
   c. feels supported in her new home

E. Read about a Canadian couple that suddenly received a lot of money. Answer the questions according to what you learned in the listening. Discuss your answers with a partner.

Allen and Violet Large received more than 11 million dollars in 2010. The Larges lived in Nova Scotia, Canada, and were in their 70s. Violet was getting treatment for cancer at the time. They didn't go on a spending spree. They decided to give their money away to family, charities, and even the hospital where Violet was treated. Married for 36 years, the Larges didn't need the money. Violet said, "What you never had, you never miss." As Allen said, "We have each other."

1. How do most people respond to receiving money? How did the Larges respond differently?

_____

_____

2. Would the Larges be happier if they spent the money? Why or why not?

_____

_____

F. **VOCABULARY** Use the new vocabulary from Listening 1. Read the paragraphs. Then fill in the blanks with the correct words from the box.

acquire *(v.)*	destructive *(adj.)*	immediate *(adj.)*
circumstances *(n.)*	dramatic *(adj.)*	pleasure *(n.)*
complicated *(adj.)*	get used to *(phr.)*	wear off *(phr. v.)*

A Success Story?

Thomas Carter never believed that he would _____ 12 million dollars, but in 2004, that's exactly what happened. He didn't receive the money from his parents—he got it when he sold an antique vase from his attic. At the time, he only had $213 in his bank account. Tom's sudden wealth brought him a lot of _____, because he could buy whatever he wanted. But this _____ improvement did not last long. He started to change his life in significant ways. These _____ changes were hard for Tom to deal with, because everything in his life became so different. Within three months, Tom had spent almost all his millions on a restaurant, a used-car lot, and an airplane. His _____ had changed, but he still had trouble managing his money.

Over the next eight years, many things started happening that Tom didn't understand. His life, which had once seemed simple, was becoming more and more _____. The effects of his wealth soon became _____; it damaged many of his relationships with friends and family members. Like many people who _____ spending a lot of money, Tom couldn't stop even after he had lost so much of it. He continued to buy houses, cars, motorcycles, and boats. The good feeling he got from spending money started to _____ as time passed. Tom told people later that he was happier before he made all that money.

 G. Go online for more practice with the vocabulary.

SAY WHAT YOU THINK

Discuss the questions in a group.

1. Which of the effects mentioned in Listening 1 do you think are the most difficult to deal with? Why?

2. Has sudden money made anyone you know about happier or unhappier? Explain.

3. Under what circumstances do you think money could make someone happier?

Signposts are words and phrases that can tell you the order in which things happened. Listen for signposts to help you follow the order of events and the logic in a text.

Listen to these examples of signposts from Listening 1.

> **First**, it affects how our brains work, at least for a while.
> **In the beginning**, when we get the money, our brain identifies it as pleasure.
> **Then** that feeling wears off.

Here are some words and phrases which are used as signposts.

At the start	In the middle	At the end
At first,	After (that),	Finally,
First,	Before (that),	In conclusion,
In the beginning,	Later,	In summary,
	Next,	
	Second,	
	Then,	

A. Listen to a reporter interview a secretary who suddenly acquired a lot of money. Complete the interview with the signposts you hear.

Reporter: You are one of many people in this town who suddenly acquired a lot of wealth when your company was purchased by a large software company. How has that affected your life?

Laura Green: Well, _____ it was pretty incredible. It took a
                    1
while for me to believe it. But _____ I began to realize what
                                2
it could actually do to my life. Things have changed dramatically.

Reporter: In what way?

Laura: I paid off all of my credit card debt. And sent my son to college.
Receiving this money was just fantastic! _____, I was
                                          3
worried all the time.

Reporter: So your financial circumstances have improved. What else
has changed?

Laura: You know, I was a secretary at that company for 20 years. I had gotten
used to just working to pay the bills. I always wished I could do more with
my life. _____ I can do that.
          4

Reporter: And what do you want to do?

Laura: _____, I'm going to go to Paris. I've always dreamed of
            5
going there. _____, I'm thinking of going back to school. I'd
              6
like to study gardening. I love flowers. _____, maybe I will
                                          7
open my own business.

Reporter: We hear stories in the news all the time about people who get a
lot of money suddenly and have many problems. How do you think those
problems can be avoided?

Laura: It's about staying true to your values and remembering what's really
important in life. You don't need to let money complicate things.

B. Answer the questions using signposts and complete sentences. Then take turns asking and answering the questions with a partner.

1. What did Laura do before she received the money?

   Before that, she worked as a secretary.

2. How did Laura feel about the money in the beginning?

   _____

3. What is one of the first things she did with the money?

   _____

4. What did she do after that?

   _____

5. What is Laura going to do in the immediate future?

   _____

6. What will she do next?

   _____

 C. Go online for more practice listening for signposts.

You are going to listen to an interview with Sonja Lyubomirsky, a psychologist who does research on happiness. As you listen to the interview, gather information and ideas about money and happiness.

PREVIEW THE LISTENING

Sonja Lyubomirsky

A. PREVIEW Which topics do you think psychologist Sonja Lyubomirsky will discuss?

☐ hobbies   ☐ travel

☐ income   ☐ where people live

☐ relationships   ☐ work

B. VOCABULARY Read aloud these words from Listening 2. Check (✓) the ones you know. Use a dictionary to define any new or unknown words. Then discuss with a partner how the words will relate to the unit.

analysis *(n.)* 🔑	**independence** *(n.)* 🔑
associated with *(adj. + prep.)* 🔑	**outcome** *(n.)*
burn out *(phr. v.)*	**persuasive** *(adj.)*
conduct *(v.)* 🔑	**somewhat** *(adv.)* 🔑
demonstrate *(v.)* 🔑	**wholly** *(adv.)*

 Oxford 3000™ words

C. Go online to listen and practice your pronunciation.

WORK WITH THE LISTENING

A. LISTEN AND TAKE NOTES Listen to the interview. Write the phrases in the correct boxes to complete the cause-effect chain.

more successful at job

- better work environment
- the happier we are
- higher income

B. Listen to the interview again. Circle the best answer to the questions.

1. How did Lyubomirsky's research influence her ideas about happiness?
   a. Her research proved that our personal relationships have the greatest influence on our happiness.
   b. Although she expected relationships to influence our happiness, her research showed that work was more important.
   c. Her research showed that wealth influenced happiness more than work.

2. What qualities in a job are associated with greater happiness?
   a. productivity, creativity, and independence
   b. structure, routine, and a pleasant environment
   c. friends, a high income, and good benefits

3. What is the relationship between happiness and income?
   a. The more money we have, the happier we will be.
   b. The happier we are, the less we care about money.
   c. Happiness, job satisfaction, and income influence each other in a positive way.

C. Read the statements. Write *T* (true) or *F* (false). Then correct each false statement to make it true.

_____ 1. Lyubomirsky and her colleagues looked at the research from 300 studies.

_____

_____ 2. Lyubomirsky has changed her ideas about what makes us happy.

_____

_____ 3. Our jobs have more of an effect on happiness than our personal relationships do.

_____

_____ 4. Happy people take fewer sick days than unhappy people.

_____

_____ 5. People who are happy when they are young will have lower salaries when they are older.

_____

_____ 6. Creativity and productivity at work leads to happier workers.

_____

D. Show the relationship between each pair. Use a plus sign (+) if there is a positive relationship, or a minus sign (−) if there is a negative relationship. Use Ø if there is no relationship between the two.

1. high creativity in a job _+_ job satisfaction

2. a job that's the same every day ____ job satisfaction

3. higher income ____ happiness

4. happiness ____ sick days

5. happiness ____ burn out

6. happiness at 18 ____ quality of job at 26

7. happiness at 18 ____ size of apartment at 30

8. happiness at 21 ____ higher income at 37

iQ ONLINE **E.** Go online to listen to *Counterfeit Money* and check your comprehension.

Vocabulary Skill Review

In Unit 1, you learned that suffixes help you recognize parts of speech. Look at the sentences in Activity F. Underline the common suffixes that indicate nouns, verbs, adjectives, and adverbs.

F. VOCABULARY Use the new vocabulary from Listening 2. Read the sentences. Then write each bold word or phrase next to the correct definition.

1. The **analysis** of the research shows that money doesn't make people happier.

2. Sudden wealth is **associated with** stress. Many people who become rich quickly experience a lot of stress.

3. I have been working too much lately. I'm afraid I'm going to **burn out**.

4. The researchers are going to **conduct** a study on money and happiness. The study will involve fifty people.

5. Mia likes a job with **independence**. She doesn't like someone telling her what to do.

6. Researchers used the results of their study to **demonstrate** that more money does not make people happier.

7. One **outcome** of sudden wealth is a change in relationships. Others include stress and loneliness.

8. The salesman was very **persuasive**. I bought the first car he showed me!

9. I'm **somewhat** unhappy at work, but not so much that I plan to quit my job.

10. I was **wholly** to blame for the argument. You did nothing wrong.

a. _____ *(n.)* the state of being free and not controlled by another person

b. _____ *(adv.)* completely; fully

c. _____ (v.) to show clearly that something exists or is true; to prove something

d. _____ (n.) the careful examination of something

e. _____ (phr. v.) to become very tired through overwork

f. _____ (v.) to do, carry out, or organize something

g. _____ (adj. + prep.) connected to; involved with

h. _____ (n.) a result or effect of an action or event

i. _____ (adj.) able to make someone do or believe something

j. _____ (adv.) a little

 G. Go online for more practice with the vocabulary.

 ## SAY WHAT YOU THINK

A. Discuss the questions in a group.

1. Which do you think comes first, happiness or money? Explain.

2. What qualities of a happy person do you think lead to better employment and financial outcomes?

B. Before you watch the video, discuss the questions in a group.

1. How much money or income do you think is necessary to be happy?

2. What are the best ways to help the poor?

 C. Go online to watch a video about how microloans, or very small loans, can help the poor. Then check your comprehension.

collateral (n.) property or something valuable that you plan to give to someone if you cannot pay back money that you borrow

creditworthy (adj.) able to be trusted to pay back money that is owed

hustle (v.) sell something

profound (adj.) very great

taken hold (phr.) become strong

welfare (n.) money the government pays regularly to people who are poor, sick, unemployed, etc.

VIDEO VOCABULARY

Critical Thinking **Tip**

Question 1 of Activity D asks you to **choose** between two things. To make the best choice, you evaluate a variety of factors, including your knowledge and experience.

D. Think about the unit video, Listening 1, and Listening 2 as you discuss the questions.

1. What is the difference between sudden wealth and earning more money from a better job? Which would you prefer? Why?

2. How responsible do you think people are for their own wealth or lack of money? How much responsibility do the rich have to help the poor?

Vocabulary Skill | Idioms

Idioms are phrases that have a different meaning than the literal meanings of the individual words. Look at these examples.

Out of the blue, Pauline found a plastic bottle.

Out of the blue means "unexpectedly." For example, storms from a clear blue sky are unexpected.

Communicating with a new friend from another state **is a snap** these days, thanks to the Internet and e-mail.

To *be a snap* means "to be really easy." For example, making a *snapping* noise with your fingers is really easy.

Learning idioms is an important way to increase your vocabulary. English speakers use them often. As you become more familiar with idioms, you will be able to understand conversations, television programs, and radio broadcasts better.

A. Work with a partner. Read the sentences. Then match each bold phrase with the correct definition.

_____ 1. I hope you have a great summer. **Drop me a line** sometime and tell me how you are doing.

_____ 2. Mark seems very upset. I think he has something he needs to **get off his chest**.

_____ 3. **Off the top of my head**, I don't have any ideas about what we should do.

_____ 4. Sometimes I can't **hold my tongue**. I always want to say what I'm feeling.

_____ 5. I'm **all ears**. How did your conversation with Professor Elliot go? I want to hear every detail!

a. listening carefully

b. without thinking first

c. to keep quiet; not to say anything

d. to talk about a problem

e. to write someone a letter

 **for Success**

If you know all
the words in a
phrase, but still
don't understand
the meaning, the
phrase might be
an idiom. Idioms
have to be learned
by experience.

B. Complete the conversations with the idioms from Activity A. Then practice the conversations with a partner.

1. **A:** I have to do a report. Where can I find out about languages that are dying out?

   B: Hmm. I don't know _____ but we can look online.

2. **A:** I can't _____ anymore. I just have to say something.

   B: That's probably not a good idea. I think you should keep quiet.

3. **A:** I can't wait for my vacation. I've never been to Australia.

   B: Oh, you'll have a great time. _____ when you can, so I know how your trip is going.

4. **A:** I have something really interesting to tell you.

   B: What is it? I'm _____ .

5. **A:** Listen, I've got something I've got to _____ . I'm really upset about it.

   B: What is it? Tell me what's wrong.

 C. Go online for more practice using idioms.

Uluru, Australia

UNIT OBJECTIVE ▶▶▶▶ At the end of this unit, you will participate in a group discussion evaluating the influence money has on happiness. Make sure to use appropriate phrases for agreeing and disagreeing when you discuss this topic.

Grammar   Types of sentences

In English, there are four main sentence types in normal speech.

Declarative sentence (a statement): I am trying to save money.
Interrogative sentence (a question): How do you save money?
Imperative sentence (a direction or command): Save your money.
Exclamatory sentence (an exclamation): I saved so much money!

Punctuation at the end of sentences

Use periods with declarative sentences, question marks with interrogative sentences, and exclamation marks with exclamatory sentences.

Imperative sentences can end with either a period or an exclamation mark. An exclamation mark shows more emotion.

A. Read the conversation. Write the sentence type (declarative, interrogative, imperative, exclamatory) next to each sentence. Then practice the conversation with a partner.

_____ 1. **Hong:** There are so many cars here!

_____ 2. **Nan:** Yeah, I know. It's hard to believe we can finally afford a new one.

_____ 3. **Hong:** I'm just glad we got the money as a reward for helping someone.

_____ 4. **Nan:** Me, too. I didn't even know your uncle very well.

_____ 5. **Hong:** Didn't you meet him at the wedding?

_____ 6. **Nan:** Yes, but I only had a short conversation with him.

_____ 7. **Hong:** I had no idea that he was going to give us so much money.

_____ 8. **Nan:** Speaking of money, hold my purse for a minute. I can't find my wallet!

B. Go online for more practice with sentence types.

C. Go online for the grammar expansion.

Intonation in different types of sentences

Intonation varies according to **sentence type**. Learning intonation patterns can help you understand if a speaker is asking a question, giving a command, or making a statement.

Declarative and imperative sentences:

Declarative and imperative sentences have a falling intonation.

I am going to purchase a new home.

Please give me some advice.

Exclamatory sentences:

Exclamatory sentences have a rise-fall intonation.

This is fun!

Interrogative sentences:

Remember that interrogative sentences or questions have two intonation patterns. *Yes/no* questions have a rising intonation pattern.

Are you coming with me?

Wh- questions have a falling intonation pattern.

Why did you leave?

A. Listen to the sentences. Check (✓) the type of sentence for each according to the intonation you hear.

1. a. ☐ statement   ☐ *yes/no* question
   b. ☐ statement   ☐ *yes/no* question

2. a. ☐ command   ☐ *wh-* question
   b. ☐ command   ☐ *wh-* question

3. a. ☐ statement   ☐ exclamation
   b. ☐ statement   ☐ exclamation

B. Listen again. Repeat the sentences using the same intonation that you hear.

iQ ONLINE **C.** Go online for more practice with intonation in different types of sentences.

Speaking Skill | **Agreeing and disagreeing**

There are certain phrases used for **agreeing and disagreeing**. It's important to know which phrases and expressions are appropriate for formal and informal situations. An informal conversation is very different from a formal discussion at college or at work.

Here are some phrases you can use when you want to agree or disagree in different situations.

Agreeing		Disagreeing
I agree (completely).	formal	I disagree.
That's exactly what I think.		I don't agree (at all).
That's a good point.		Sorry, but that's not my opinion.
That's right.		I don't feel the same way.
I think so too.		I don't think so.
Absolutely!		No way!
Yeah, I know!	informal	Oh, come on!

A. Listen to the conversations. Complete each conversation with the phrases you hear.

1. **Ellie:** What are you going to do with the money your grandfather gave you?

   Sam: I'm not sure. I think I'm going to take an expensive vacation.

   Ellie: Really? Don't you have a lot of school loans to pay?

   Sam: _____. Maybe the vacation's not such a good idea.

1

   Ellie: _____! Vacations are fun, but it's much more

2

   important to pay off your debt.

2. **Monica:** I think raising the average income in countries around the world

   is the best way to increase the level of happiness.

   Patricia: I _____. More money might make the very poor

3

   happier, but not everyone.

Monica: I _____. I think everyone except perhaps the very
4
wealthy will benefit from a higher income.

Patricia: Well, I can see we'll just have to agree to disagree.

 B. Go online for more practice with agreeing and disagreeing.

Note-taking Skill | Taking and organizing notes from a discussion

Sometimes it is important to take notes from a pair or group discussion. You may need to report on the discussion to the class, or you may want to use the ideas from the discussion to prepare for a test, write an essay, or make a presentation. One way to organize your notes is by using a graphic organizer. For a pair discussion, you can use a Venn diagram. This allows you to show points of agreement and disagreement.

A. With a partner, read this excerpt from a discussion about happiness. Then take notes in the Venn diagram on page 170.

Tom: OK. What do we want to say about the research on money and happiness?

Marc: Well, according to the study by Betsey Stevenson and Jeffrey Wolfers, richer people are happier. I know when I have more money, I feel more relaxed about paying my bills.

Tom: True. But didn't research in the U.K. by Layard show that as long as you have a certain amount, you can be happy? All I want is to be able to pay all my bills and have some extra to do the things I enjoy. I don't need a really big house or an expensive car.

Marc: I agree. I need a home and a car, but they don't have to be really huge or expensive. But I do want to have enough money to travel. And when I say travel, I mean, to places I've never been—like Chiang Mai in Thailand and Machu Picchu in Peru. And I don't want to skimp. I want to really enjoy the trip and stay in nice hotels.

Tom: Yeah, I would love to go to those places. But I don't need to stay in nice hotels. I could camp or stay in hostels. The important thing is the people you are with and the experiences you have.

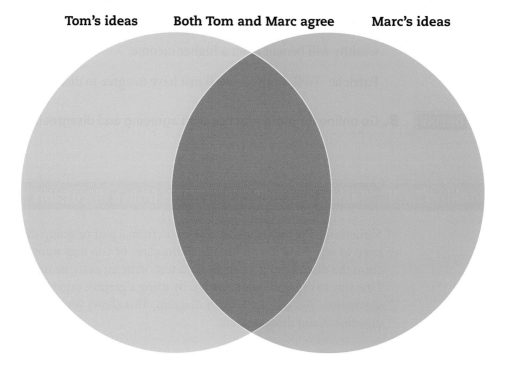

Tom's ideas   **Both Tom and Marc agree**   **Marc's ideas**

B. Use your notes to answer the questions.

1. What was the topic of the discussion? _____

2. What information did they give to support their ideas?

   _____

   _____

3. What did the two speakers agree about?

   _____

   _____

4. What did they disagree about?

   _____

   _____

C. With a partner, summarize the speakers' points using the notes from the graphic organizer.

 D. Go online for more practice taking and organizing notes from a discussion.

In this assignment, you are going to take part in a group discussion about money and happiness. As you prepare for the discussion, think about the Unit Question, "Can money buy happiness?" Use information from Listening 1, Listening 2, the unit video, and your work in this unit to support your discussion. Refer to the Self-Assessment checklist on page 172.

CONSIDER THE IDEAS

Work with a partner. Discuss the questions about money and happiness. Be sure to use the correct intonation when you ask each other questions.

What is money's influence on happiness?

What kind of person do you think would be happier with more money? Why?

Would your life be different if you had more or less money? How?

Is it more enjoyable to give or receive money? Why?

PREPARE AND SPEAK

Tip for Success

When disagreeing with someone, you can sound more polite by starting with *I know what you mean, but …* or *I see your point, but …*

A. **GATHER IDEAS** **Take notes on your discussion with your partner. Use these questions to guide you.**

1. What were the main points of your discussion?

2. What did you agree on?

3. What did you disagree on?

B. **ORGANIZE IDEAS** **Choose one question from the Consider the Ideas activity. Use the outline to help you prepare for a group discussion. Do not write exactly what you are going to say. Just write notes to help you organize your ideas.**

Question: _____

Ideas that I agree with:

_____

_____

Ideas that I disagree with:

_____

_____

My answer to the question:

_____

_____

Reasons for my answer:

_____

_____

Examples:

_____

_____

C. SPEAK Work in a group. Take turns presenting your ideas on the questions you chose in Activity B. Refer to the Self-Assessment checklist below before you begin.

 Go online for your alternate Unit Assignment.

CHECK AND REFLECT

A. CHECK Think about the Unit Assignment as you complete the Self-Assessment checklist.

SELF-ASSESSMENT		
Yes	No	
☐	☐	I was able to speak easily about the topic.
☐	☐	My group understood me.
☐	☐	I used vocabulary from the unit.
☐	☐	I used different types of sentences when speaking.
☐	☐	I used different intonation patterns.
☐	☐	I used phrases to agree and disagree.

B. REFLECT Go to the Online Discussion Board to discuss these questions.

1. What is something new you learned in this unit?

2. Look back at the Unit Question—Can money buy happiness? Is your answer different now than when you started this unit? If yes, how is it different? Why?

TRACK YOUR SUCCESS

Circle the words and phrases you have learned in this unit.

Nouns
analysis 🔑 AWL
circumstances 🔑 AWL
independence 🔑
outcome AWL
pleasure 🔑

Verbs
acquire 🔑 AWL
conduct 🔑 AWL
demonstrate 🔑 AWL
inherit

Adjectives
associated (with) 🔑
complicated 🔑
destructive
dramatic 🔑 AWL
immediate 🔑
persuasive

Adverbs
Absolutely! 🔑
Finally, 🔑 AWL
First, 🔑
Later, 🔑
Next, 🔑
Second, 🔑
somewhat 🔑 AWL
Then, 🔑
wholly

Phrasal Verbs
burn out
wear off

Phrases
After (that),
At first,
Before (that),
get used to

I agree (completely).
I disagree.
I don't agree (at all).
I don't feel the same way.
I don't think so.
I think so too.
In conclusion,
In summary,
In the beginning,
No way!
Oh, come on!
Sorry, but that's not my
    opinion.
That's a good point.
That's exactly what I
    think.
That's right.
Yeah, I know!

🔑 Oxford 3000™ words
AWL Academic Word List

Check (✓) the skills you learned. If you need more work on a skill, refer to the page(s) in parentheses.

LISTENING ◼	I can listen for signposts. (p. 157)
VOCABULARY ◼	I can use idioms. (p. 164)
GRAMMAR ◼	I can use different types of sentences. (p. 166)
PRONUNCIATION ◼	I can use correct intonation in different types of sentences. (p. 167)
SPEAKING ◼	I can use phrases for agreeing and disagreeing. (p. 168)
NOTE TAKING ◼	I can take and organize notes from a discussion. (p. 169)
**UNIT OBJECTIVE** ▶▶▶▶	◼ I can gather information and ideas to participate in a group discussion evaluating the influence money has on happiness.

Q

What can we learn from success and failure?

A Discuss these questions with your classmates.

1. What are some of the different ways a person can be successful?

2. In what ways do you think you are successful?

3. Look at the photo. What is happening? In what ways can failure affect people?

174

UNIT ▶▶▶▶
OBJECTIVE

Listen to a lecture and a speech and gather information
and ideas to discuss successful and unsuccessful
personal experiences and explain what you learned
from them.

B Listen to *The Q Classroom* online. Then answer
these questions.

1. What types of success do the students mention?
Do you agree or disagree with their ideas? Why?

2. Marcus thinks we learn more from our failures than
our successes. What explanation does he give for
this opinion? Do you agree?

iQ ONLINE **C** Go online to watch a video about a race car driver.
Then check your comprehension.

blown away *(adj.)* impressed by
someone or something

mayhem *(n.)* confusion

pit crews *(n.)* teams of people that work
on race cars

tinker *(v.)* repair things

VIDEO VOCABULARY

iQ ONLINE **D** Go to the Online Discussion Board to discuss the
Unit Question with your classmates.

E Look at the questionnaire. Check (✓) the three things that are most true for you. Then write reasons for each of your choices.

What Does Success Mean to You?

For Me Success Means …	Reasons:
☐ being rich	
☐ doing well on exams	
☐ having a job I love	
☐ enjoying a happy family life	
☐ being able to do what I want	
☐ having lots of friends	
☐ enjoying good health	
☐ being famous	
☐ having a powerful or important job	

Your idea: _____

Your idea: _____

F Discuss your answers in a group. Explain the reasons for your choices.

LISTENING 1 | Chasing Your Dreams

UNIT OBJECTIVE ▶▶▶▶ You are going to listen to the beginning of a lecture by a college professor. As you listen to the lecture, gather information and ideas about what we can learn from success and failure.

PREVIEW THE LISTENING

A college professor is talking about the importance of success and what it means to be successful.

A. **PREVIEW** Which things do you think the college professor will say are important for success? Check (✓) your answers.

☐ being lucky

☐ having clear goals

☐ never giving up

☐ trying hard

B. **VOCABULARY** Read aloud these words from Listening 1. Check (✓) the ones you know. Use a dictionary to define any new or unknown words. Then discuss with a partner how the words will relate to the unit.

achieve *(v.)* 🔑	**goal** *(n.)* 🔑
determination *(n.)* 🔑	**measure** *(v.)* 🔑
downside *(n.)*	**realistic** *(adj.)* 🔑
frustrating *(adj.)*	**ruin** *(v.)* 🔑
give up *(phr. v.)*	**status** *(n.)* 🔑

🔑 Oxford 3000™ words

iQ **ONLINE** **C.** Go online to listen and practice your pronunciation.

WORK WITH THE LISTENING

A. **LISTEN AND TAKE NOTES** Listen to the lecture. Complete the missing words in the chart, and add notes on any examples the professor gives.

Main points	Examples
1. Make sure your goals are _____.	
2. Aiming for success should not cause _____ or _____.	none given
3. Success can bring _____.	
4. Our definition of success changes with _____.	

B. In what ways does the professor use humor to make her points? Do you think this is an effective technique? Why or why not?

C. Listen to the lecture again. Circle the answer that best completes each statement according to what the professor says.

1. We learn that success is good _____.
   a. from an early age
   b. as we grow older

2. To be successful, you _____.
   a. need to set achievable goals
   b. should never stop trying to achieve your goals

3. Achieving your goals should be _____.
   a. the most important thing in your life
   b. one of several important things in your life

4. You should try to focus on _____.
   a. only the positive aspects of success
   b. both the positive and the negative aspects of success

5. You need to _____.
   a. keep the same goals throughout your life
   b. change your goals to match different stages in your life

D. Read the statements. Write *T* (true) or *F* (false). Then correct each false statements to make it true.

_____ 1. This is the professor's first lecture on success to the class.

_____ 2. She says that with hard work and determination, it is possible to achieve anything you want.

_____ 3. According to the professor, trying to achieve some dreams can be a waste of time and effort.

_____ 4. The professor says that trying too hard to be successful can cause problems.

_____ 5. She argues that success can also bring failure.

_____ 6. She says that people often see success differently as they grow older.

Vocabulary Skill Review

Remember to read the whole sentence and consider the *context*. This can help you identify the correct word and meaning.

E. **VOCABULARY** Use the new vocabulary from Listening 1. Read the sentences. Circle the answer that best matches the meaning of each bold word or phrase.

1. It may be difficult to **achieve** your dreams, but hard work can often help you get what you want from life.
    a. reach   b. control   c. remember

2. **Determination** is important for success. You have to keep trying even when it is difficult.
    a. force   b. willpower   c. luck

3. I love my job, but the **downside** is that the salary is low.
    a. mistake   b. error   c. disadvantage

4. It can be very **frustrating** to try hard without succeeding.
    a. difficult   b. boring   c. annoying

5. "If at first you don't succeed, try, try again." This saying means "don't **give up**".
    a. quit   b. fail   c. alter

6. Peter is a salesperson now, but his **goal** is to have his own business someday.
    a. argument   b. ambition   c. challenge

7. There are various ways to **measure** success. It's not just about making lots of money.
    a. judge   b. enjoy   c. discuss

8. It's not **realistic** to expect to be successful at everything you do. No one can be good at everything.
   a. confident   b. reasonable   c. intelligent

9. Don't wash that sweater in hot water. You'll **ruin** it.
   a. break   b. injure   c. spoil

10. Sarah's new job gave her a much higher **status** within the company.
    a. position   b. activity   c. popularity

 F. Go online for more practice with the vocabulary.

 ## SAY WHAT YOU THINK

Discuss the questions in a group.

1. Do you agree with the points the professor makes about success? Why or why not?

2. Who is the most successful person you know? In what ways is he or she successful?

3. What things do you think are more important than success?

There are many different types of success.

Listening for examples

Listening for examples will help you understand a speaker's main points more clearly. Speakers often introduce examples with a common phrase that tells you that an example follows.

| For example, | such as | To give (you) an example, |
| For instance, | Take, for example, | To illustrate this, |

A. Listen to the lecture again. List the phrases the professor uses to introduce examples.

_____

_____

_____

_____

B. Listen to Paul talk about how his view of success has changed. List each example he gives. You do not need to write full sentences.

1. When he was younger, Paul says he was "money hungry."

   Example: _____

2. He also says he was concerned about status.

   Example: _____

3. These days, Paul says being successful for him means being healthy.

   Example: _____

4. He also says that having good friends is important to him.

   Example: _____

C. Think about one goal you would like to achieve. Write three benefits you expect from achieving this goal.

Your goal: _____

Benefits:

1. _____

   _____

2. _____

   _____

3. _____

   _____

D. Work with a partner. Take turns talking about your goals and their benefits. Use phrases from the Listening Skill box on page 180 when you give examples. Take notes below as you listen to your partner. Then discuss whether or not you agree with the benefits she or he expects.

Your partner's goal: _____

Benefits:

1. _____
   _____

2. _____
   _____

3. _____
   _____

 **E.** Go online for more practice listening for examples.

LISTENING 2 | The Benefits of Failure

UNIT OBJECTIVE ▶▶▶ You are going to listen to a short speech by a college student. As you listen to the speech, gather information and ideas about what we can learn from success and failure.

PREVIEW THE LISTENING

A. **PREVIEW** Carl Simmons, a college student, is talking about the opposite of success—failure. In what ways do you think failure can be a positive experience? Make a list of your ideas, and then compare with a partner.

_____

_____

B. VOCABULARY Read aloud these words from Listening 2. Check (✓) the ones you know. Use a dictionary to define any new or unknown words. Then discuss with a partner how the words will relate to the unit.

develop *(v.)* 🔑	**lack** *(v.)* 🔑	**top** *(adj.)* 🔑
emphasize *(v.)* 🔑	**permit** *(v.)* 🔑	**turn down** *(phr. v.)*
fear *(v.)* 🔑	**preparation** *(n.)* 🔑	

🔑 Oxford 3000™ words

 C. Go online to listen and practice your pronunciation.

WORK WITH THE LISTENING

 A. LISTEN AND TAKE NOTES Listen to Carl's speech. Complete the two main points he makes. Then complete the examples he gives to support his opinion.

1. **Main point 1:** We shouldn't be _____ of failure. We can _____ from our mistakes.

2. **Main point 2:** Don't let failure _____ you. Never give up!

Akio Morita

Examples of people who failed but went on to succeed	
Stephen King	_____ publishers turned down his first book
Michael Jordan	_____ from his high school basketball team
John Grisham	his first book, *A _____ to Kill*, was a failure
Akio Morita	first product was a _____ that didn't work
Thomas Edison	struggled to make the first _____ work

B. Listen to the speech again. Match the people with the statements about them.

___ 1. Stephen King   a. threw his first book in the trash

___ 2. Michael Jordan   b. failed thousands of times before succeeding

___ 3. John Grisham   c. lost a lot of money at first

___ 4. Akio Morita   d. was rejected by 16 agents and publishers

___ 5. Thomas Edison   e. "lacked skill"

C. Check (✓) the main ideas of the speech.

___ 1. Some people prefer to fail rather than succeed.

___ 2. It is sometimes necessary to fail in order to succeed.

___ 3. Modern society doesn't accept failure.

___ 4. We can learn from our failures.

___ 5. Many successful people begin by failing.

D. Complete the summary.

Carl Simmons' view is that failure is something we all

_____, but in fact it is an important stage on the road

to _____. He says we can learn a lot more from our

failures than we can from our successes. Failure is something to be

_____ by. It is a good _____ for life. We need

to experience failure, and _____ from it, in order to succeed.

E. Go online to listen to *The Advantages of Business Failure* and check your comprehension.

F. **VOCABULARY** Use the new vocabulary from Listening 2. Circle the answer that best matches the meaning of each word or phrase in bold.

 for Success

Making lists of words with similar meanings, or *synonyms*, is a good way to expand your vocabulary. Use a dictionary to study differences in meaning.

1. **develop** *(v.)*	future	changing	(improve)
2. **emphasize** *(v.)*	successful	importance	stress
3. **fear** *(v.)*	scare	frightening	be afraid
4. **lack** *(v.)*	missing	absence	need
5. **permit** *(v.)*	allow	helpful	ability
6. **preparation** *(n.)*	ready	training	educate
7. **top** *(adj.)*	leading	famously	seriousness
8. **turn down** *(phr. v.)*	unhelpful	acceptance	refuse

 G. Go online for more practice with the vocabulary.

SAY WHAT YOU THINK

A. Discuss the questions in a group.

1. Of the people in Listening 2, who do you think overcame the biggest difficulties? Who learned the most from their failures?

2. Give an example of a time when you succeeded after failing at first. What did you learn from your mistakes?

B. Think about the unit video, Listening 1, and Listening 2 as you discuss the questions.

1. Do you think the examples in Carl Simmons' speech support the professor's ideas about success in Listening 1? Why or why not?

2. In what ways, if any, has your view of success and failure changed?

Prefixes are added to the beginning of words to change their meaning. Understanding prefixes can help you expand your vocabulary and figure out the meaning of unknown words.

Notice the use of prefixes in these examples from Listening 2.

> Being successful is not about being a **multi**millionaire.
> (**multi**- + millionaire = multimillionaire)
> Chasing an **im**possible dream, one that you can never reach, is a frustrating waste of time and energy. (**im**- + possible = impossible)

Many prefixes give the opposite meaning to words.

> **dis**- **dis**agree
> **im**- (before words beginning with *m/p*) **im**polite
> **ir**- (before words beginning with *r*) **ir**rational

These prefixes give other meanings to words.

> **co**- (together) **co**operate
> **re**- (again) **re**place, **re**write
> **multi**- (many) **multi**purpose
> **anti**- (against) **anti**war

A. Add a prefix from the Vocabulary Skill box to complete each word.

1. _re_ view
2. ____ responsible
3. ____ like
4. ____ worker
5. ____ perfect
6. ____ social
7. ____ national
8. ____ honest
9. ____ patient
10. ____ regular
11. ____ apply
12. ____ media

B. Choose three words from Activity A. Write a sentence using each word.

1. _____

2. _____

3. _____

C. Read your sentences to a partner. Write any words you hear from Activity A in your notebook. Underline the prefixes.

D. Go online for more practice with prefixes.

SPEAKING

At the end of this unit, you will take part in a discussion about success and failure. Make sure to ask for and give clarification as you discuss the topic.

Grammar Simple past and present perfect

Use the **simple past** for actions that began and ended in the past. For actions that began in the past and continue up to the present, use the **present perfect**.

Simple past

> Michael Jordan **played** basketball.
> (He no longer plays basketball.)

Present perfect

> John Grisham **has written** thirty novels.
> (He is still writing novels.)

Use the simple past for actions that occurred at a specific time in the past. If the time an action occurred is not known or not important, use the present perfect.

Simple past

> Stephen King **published** his first book in 1974.

Present perfect

> Stephen King **has published** many books.
> (When he published the books is not important.)

Use the present perfect for actions that happened more than once in the past when the focus is on how often the actions happened rather than when they happened.

> Carl Simmons fails sometimes. He **has learned** from his mistakes.

Time expressions used with the simple past and present perfect

Last, *ago*, *in*, and *on* are commonly used with the simple past to show that an action was completed in the past.

For and *since* are commonly used with the present perfect to show that an action is connected to the present.

> Sara started college **two years ago**.
> She has been a student **for two years**.

A. Circle the correct verb forms to complete the conversation. Then practice the conversation with a partner.

Ashley: Hey, Kevin. Great shot! You know, you're a pretty good tennis player. (<u>Did you ever enter / Have you ever entered</u>) any tennis competitions?

1

Kevin: Yes, I (<u>did / have</u>). Actually, I (<u>came / have come</u>) in second in the

2   3

Senior Tournament at our club last year.

Ashley: Really? That's great. (<u>Did you enjoy / Have you enjoyed</u>) it?

4

Kevin: Sure! Especially because it (<u>was / has been</u>) my first attempt. How

5

about you?

Ashley: Oh, I play in a small local league, but I (<u>didn't win / haven't won</u>) any

6

competitions or anything. I just play for fun, to keep fit and healthy.

B. Think of a hobby or sport that you enjoy. Note your answers to these questions. Then ask and answer the questions with a partner.

1. What hobby or sport do you enjoy? _____

2. How long have you done it? _____

3. Why do you like it? _____

4. Have you ever entered any competitions? _____

5. In what ways are you "successful" at your hobby or sport?

_____

C. Complete each statement with your own ideas. Then compare sentences with a partner.

1. I _____ lately.

2. I _____ since last week.

3. I _____ yet.

4. I _____ a few years ago.

5. I _____ yesterday.

D. Go online for more practice with simple past and present perfect.

E. Go online for the grammar expansion.

Varying intonation to maintain interest

You can help your listeners follow what you are saying more easily, and also help to keep them interested while you are speaking, by varying your intonation—making your voice rise and fall—a little more than usual.

Listen to this sentence from Carl Simmons's speech. You will hear it twice. Notice how the speaker sounds more interested the second time, and this makes it more interesting and easier to follow.

☐ Just as success is something we all want, failure is something that we all fear.

Listen to some more examples. Notice how the speaker varies her intonation to make what she says easier to follow and sound more interesting.

You can learn more from your failures than you can from your successes.

Success for my grandfather is getting out of bed in the morning!

Failing is a good preparation for life.

A. Listen twice to each sentence. Which sounds more interested, Speaker 1 or Speaker 2?

	Speaker 1	Speaker 2
1. Failure is an important stage on the road to success.	☐	☐
2. We shouldn't be afraid of failure because we can learn from it.	☐	☐
3. Failure is something to be encouraged by.	☐	☐
4. Don't give up too easily!	☐	☐

B. Listen again. Repeat the sentences, using the same intonation you hear.

C. Read the paragraph below. Think about how you can use intonation to make this sound interesting and easier for listeners to follow. With a partner, take turns reading the paragraph aloud.

You need to experience failure and learn from it, in order to really succeed. Failing is a good preparation for life. It makes you stronger and more able to overcome life's problems. Don't be scared of failure! It might sound strange, but letting go of your fear of failure might help you to succeed.

D. Listen and check your answers to Activity C. Then listen and repeat, using the same intonation.

 E. Go online for more practice varying intonation to maintain interest.

Asking for and giving clarification

After you listen to a speech or presentation, you can ask questions if you need **clarification** or more information about something the speaker said. Asking questions shows that you are interested and have been paying attention.

Asking for clarification

Sorry, I don't get what you mean.
What do you mean exactly?
Could you say a bit more about …?
Can you give an example?

After giving a speech or presentation, it is a good idea to ask the audience for questions. This gives you an opportunity to clarify your most important points and make sure your audience understood them.

Giving clarification

What I'm trying to say …
To give you an example …
I mean …

A. Listen to the excerpts from a discussion. Complete the excerpts wth the phrases you hear. Then practice the conversations with a partner.

1. **Professor:** So you need to make sure the success you're aiming for is achievable.

   Student 1: _____ .

   1

   Professor: What _____ be realistic with the goals

   2

   you set for yourself.

2. **Professor:** Success in one area can bring problems in others.

   Student 2: _____?
   ₃

   Professor: Well, _____, someone can be at the
   ₄
   top of her career, but her family life might be in crisis as a result.

3. **Professor:** Keep your desire for success in proportion.

   Student 3: _____?
   ₅

   Professor: Yes. I mean don't let your desire for success become greater
   than other important areas in your life.

4. **Professor:** Our definition of success alters with age.

   Student 1: _____?
   ₆

   Professor: Sure. Someone of 20 might view success as being rich, but at 50
   that same person might think of success as a happy family life.

B. **Work with a partner. Take turns reading the statements from Listening 1
and Listening 2 aloud and asking for and giving clarification.**

1. Failure is an important stage on the road to success.

   A: Sorry, I don't get what you mean.
   B: What I mean by that is we learn from our mistakes.

2. If at first you don't succeed, try, try again.

3. Success for my grandfather is simply getting out of bed in the morning.

4. Failing is a good preparation for life.

 C. **Go online for more practice asking for and giving clarification.**

When discussing a topic, you may want to give examples to help support your opinion. Taking notes with examples is therefore a very useful skill. It allows you to organize your ideas and support your opinions in a way that is easy to refer to when you are speaking.

Look at these main points and examples from Listening 1. Notice how the main points are noted separately, next to the supporting examples.

Main points	Examples
1. Make sure your goals are realistic.	short, 30-year-old male smoker shouldn't quit job to become basketball player
2. Aiming for success should not cause stress or anxiety.	no example
3. Success can bring problems.	• famous people (TV presenters and sports stars, etc.) who have relationship problems
	• a high school friend, successful businessman but is now divorced

A. Think of different examples to support each main point in the chart below. Then discuss the topic of success with a partner.

Main points	Examples
1. Make sure your goals are realistic.	
2. Aiming for success should not cause stress or anxiety.	
3. Success can bring problems.	

 B. Go online for more practice taking notes with examples.

In this assignment, you are going to take part in a discussion about success and failure. As you prepare for the discussion, think about the Unit Question, "What can we learn from success and failure?" Use information from Listening 1, Listening 2, the unit video, and your work in this unit to support your discussion. Refer to the Self-Assessment checklist on page 196.

CONSIDER THE IDEAS

Work with a partner. Read the quotes about success and failure. Decide what the quotes mean, and think of an example for each one. Take notes in the charts.

Critical Thinking (Tip)

This activity asks you to **paraphrase**. **Paraphrasing**, or saying the information in your own words, helps you to understand and remember ideas better.

"Success is not the key to happiness. Happiness is the key to success. If you love what you are doing, you will be successful."

—*Albert Schweitzer*

Meaning	Example

Do you agree or disagree with this quote? Explain.

_____

_____

"Success is never final. Failure is never fatal. Courage is what counts."

—*Winston Churchill*

Meaning	Example

Do you agree or disagree with this quote? Explain.

_____

_____

> "Many of life's failures are people who did not realize how close they were to success when they gave up."
>
> —*Thomas Edison*

Meaning	Example

Do you agree or disagree with this quote? Explain.

_____

_____

PREPARE AND SPEAK

A. GATHER IDEAS **Think about what success means to you. Complete the activities.**

1. Make a list of things you have been successful at. They can be big things, such as graduating from high school, or small things, such as cooking a delicious meal.

   _____

   _____

   _____

2. Now make a list of things you have tried, but were not successful at. Again, they can be big things, such as applying for a job, or small things, such as playing a game of tennis.

   _____

   _____

   _____

B. ORGANIZE IDEAS **Choose one example from each list in Activity A. Complete the outline to help you prepare to discuss your ideas.**

1. **Something I was successful at:** _____

What were some of the difficulties you experienced?

_____

_____

How has this experience affected your life?

_____

_____

What have you learned from this experience?

_____

_____

_____

2. **Something I was not successful at:** _____

What were some of the difficulties you experienced?

_____

_____

How has this experience affected your life?

_____

_____

What have you learned from this experience?

_____

_____

_____

C. SPEAK **Complete these steps. Refer to the Self-Assessment checklist below before you begin.**

1. Work with a partner. Take turns telling each other about your experiences.

2. Discuss which experience you learned more from. Do not read directly from your outline. Just use it to help you remember your ideas. Use phrases from the Speaking Skill box on page 190 to ask for and give clarification.

 Go online for your alternate Unit Assignment.

CHECK AND REFLECT

A. CHECK **Think about the Unit Assignment as you complete the Self-Assessment checklist.**

SELF-ASSESSMENT		
Yes	No	
☐	☐	I was able to speak easily about the topic.
☐	☐	My partner understood me.
☐	☐	I used vocabulary from the unit.
☐	☐	I used simple past and present perfect.
☐	☐	I varied my intonation to maintain interest.
☐	☐	I asked for and gave clarification.

B. REFLECT **Go to the Online Discussion Board to discuss these questions.**

1. What is something new you learned in this unit?

2. Look back at the Unit Question—What can we learn from success and failure? Is your answer different now than when you started this unit? If yes, how is it different? Why?

TRACK YOUR SUCCESS

Circle the words and phrases you have learned in this unit.

Nouns
determination 🔑
downside
goal 🔑 AWL
preparation 🔑
status 🔑 AWL

Verbs
achieve 🔑 AWL
develop 🔑
emphasize 🔑 AWL
fear 🔑
lack 🔑
measure 🔑
permit 🔑
ruin 🔑

Adjectives
frustrating
realistic 🔑
top 🔑

Phrasal Verbs
give up
turn down

Phrases
Can you give an example?
Could you say a bit more about …?
For example,
For instance,

Sorry, I don't get what you mean.
such as
Take, for example,
To give (you) an example,
To illustrate this,
What do you mean by …?
What I'm trying to say is …
What I mean by that is …

🔑 Oxford 3000™ words
AWL Academic Word List

Check (✓) the skills you learned. If you need more work on a skill, refer to the page(s) in parentheses.

LISTENING ☐ I can listen for examples. (p. 180)
VOCABULARY ☐ I can use prefixes. (p. 186)
GRAMMAR ☐ I can use simple past and present perfect. (p. 187)
PRONUNCIATION ☐ I can vary intonation to maintain interest. (p. 189)
SPEAKING ☐ I can ask for and give clarification. (p. 190)
NOTE TAKING ☐ I can take notes with examples. (p. 192)

UNIT OBJECTIVE  ☐ I can gather information and ideas to discuss successful and unsuccessful personal experiences and explain what I learned from them.

Audio can be found in the *iQ Online* Media Center. Go to iQOnlinePractice.com. Click on the Media Center. Choose to stream or download ⬇ the audio file you select. Not all audio files are available for download.

Authors

Miles Craven has worked in English language education since 1988, teaching in private language schools, British Council centers, and universities in Italy, Portugal, Spain, Hong Kong, Japan, and the U.K. He has a wide range of experience as a teacher, teacher trainer, examiner, course designer, and textbook writer. Miles is author or co-author of over 30 textbooks, and regularly presents at conferences around the world. He also acts as Advisor for Executive Education programs at the Møller Centre for Continuing Education Ltd., Churchill College, University of Cambridge. His research focuses on helping students develop the skills and strategies they need to become confident communicators. He currently specializes in exam preparation for the TOEIC test.

Kristin Donnalley Sherman holds an M. Ed. in TESL from the University of North Carolina, Charlotte. She has taught ESL/EFL at Central Piedmont Community College in Charlotte, North Carolina for more than fifteen years, and has taught a variety of subjects, including grammar, reading, composition, listening, and speaking. She has written student books, teacher's editions, and workbooks in the area of academic ESL/EFL. In addition, she regularly presents at conferences and workshops internationally.

Series Consultants

ONLINE INTEGRATION

Chantal Hemmi holds an Ed.D. TEFL and is a Japan-based teacher trainer and curriculum designer. Since leaving her position as Academic Director of the British Council in Tokyo, she has been teaching at the Center for Language Education and Research at Sophia University on an EAP/CLIL program offered for undergraduates. She delivers lectures and teacher trainings throughout Japan, Indonesia, and Malaysia.

COMMUNICATIVE GRAMMAR

Nancy Schoenfeld holds an M.A. in TESOL from Biola University in La Mirada, California, and has been an English language instructor since 2000. She has taught ESL in California and Hawaii, and EFL in Thailand and Kuwait. She has also trained teachers in the United States and Indonesia. Her interests include teaching vocabulary, extensive reading, and student motivation. She is currently an English Language Instructor at Kuwait University.

WRITING

Marguerite Ann Snow holds a Ph.D. in Applied Linguistics from UCLA. She teaches in the TESOL M.A. program in the Charter College of Education at California State University, Los Angeles. She was a Fulbright scholar in Hong Kong and Cyprus. In 2006, she received the President's Distinguished Professor award at Cal State, LA. She has trained EFL teachers in Algeria, Argentina, Brazil, Egypt, Libya, Morocco, Pakistan, Peru, Spain, and Turkey. She is the author/editor of publications in the areas of integrated content, English for academic purposes, and standards for English teaching and learning. She recently served as a co-editor of *Teaching English as a Second or Foreign Language* (4th ed.).

VOCABULARY

Cheryl Boyd Zimmerman is a Professor at California State University, Fullerton. She specializes in second-language vocabulary acquisition, an area in which she is widely published. She teaches graduate courses on second-language acquisition, culture, vocabulary, and the fundamentals of TESOL and is a frequent invited speaker on topics related to vocabulary teaching and learning. She is the author of *Word Knowledge: A Vocabulary Teacher's Handbook* and Series Director of *Inside Reading, Inside Writing,* and *Inside Listening and Speaking,* all published by Oxford University Press.

ASSESSMENT

Lawrence J. Zwier holds an M.A. in TESL from the University of Minnesota. He is currently the Associate Director for Curriculum Development at the English Language Center at Michigan State University in East Lansing. He has taught ESL/EFL in the United States, Saudi Arabia, Malaysia, Japan, and Singapore.

iQ ONLINE extends your learning beyond the classroom. This online content is specifically designed for you! *iQ Online* **gives you flexible access to essential content.**

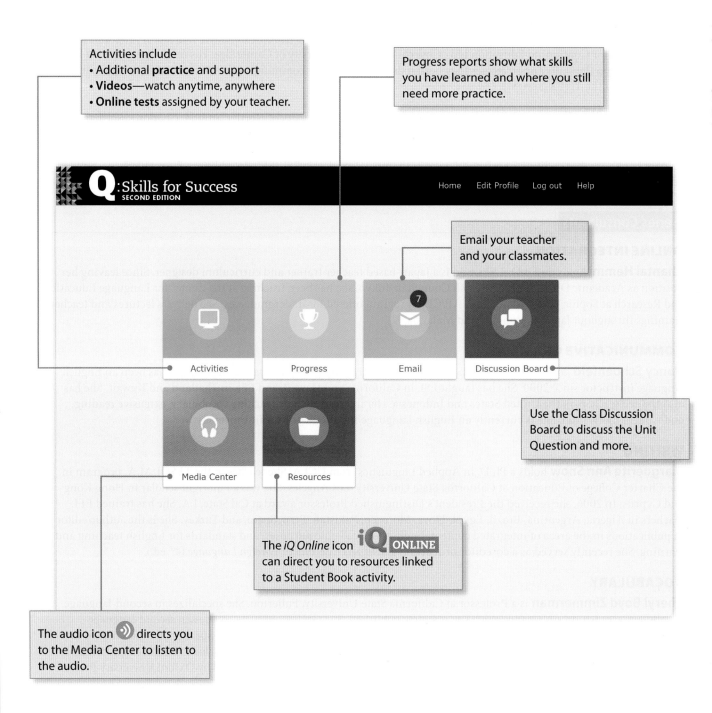

Activities include
- Additional **practice** and support
- **Videos**—watch anytime, anywhere
- **Online tests** assigned by your teacher.

Progress reports show what skills you have learned and where you still need more practice.

Email your teacher and your classmates.

Use the Class Discussion Board to discuss the Unit Question and more.

The *iQ Online* icon **iQ ONLINE** can direct you to resources linked to a Student Book activity.

The audio icon directs you to the Media Center to listen to the audio.

SEE THE INSIDE FRONT COVER FOR HOW TO REGISTER FOR *iQ ONLINE* FOR THE FIRST TIME.

Take Control of Your Learning

You have the choice of where and how you complete the activities. Access your activities and view your progress at any time.

Your teacher may

- assign *iQ Online* as homework,
- do the activities with you in class, or
- let you complete the activities at a pace that is right for you.

iQ Online makes it easy to access everything you need.

Set Clear Goals

STEP 1 If it is your first time, look through the site. See what learning opportunities are available.

STEP 2 The Student Book provides the framework and purpose for each online activity. Before going online, notice the goal of the exercises you are going to do.

STEP 3 Stay on top of your work, following the teacher's instructions.

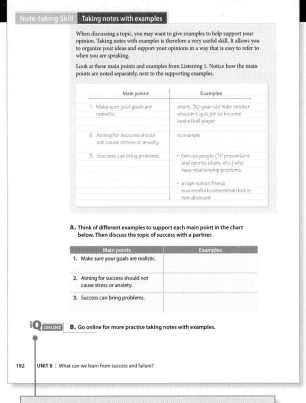

Notice the icon. It directs you to the online materials linked to the Student Book activities.

STEP 4 Use *iQ Online* for review. You can use the materials any time. It is easy for you to do follow-up activities when you have missed a class or want to review.

Manage Your Progress

The activities in *iQ Online* are designed for you to work independently. You can become a confident learner by monitoring your progress and reviewing the activities at your own pace. You may already be used to working online, but if you are not, go to your teacher for guidance.

Check 'View Reports' to monitor your progress. The reports let you track your own progress at a glance. Think about your own performance and set new goals that are right for you, following the teacher's instructions.

iQ Online is a research-based solution specifically designed for English language learners that extends learning beyond the classroom. I hope these steps help you make the most of this essential content.

Chantal Hemmi, EdD TEFL
Center for Language Education and Research
Sophia University, Japan

The keywords of the **Oxford 3000**™ have been carefully selected by a group of language experts and experienced teachers as the words which should receive priority in vocabulary study because of their importance and usefulness.

AWL **The Academic Word List** is the most principled and widely accepted list of academic words. Averil Coxhead gathered information from academic materials across the academic disciplines to create this word list.

The Common European Framework of Reference for Languages (CEFR) provides a basic description of what language learners have to do to use language effectively. The system contains 6 reference levels: **A1**, **A2**, **B1**, **B2**, **C1**, **C2**. CEFR leveling provided by the Word Family Framework, created by Richard West and published by the British Council. http://www.learnenglish.org.uk/wff/

UNIT 1

assume (v.) 🔑 AWL, A1
behavior (n.) 🔑, A1
briefly (adv.) 🔑, B1
conscious (adj.) 🔑, A2
effective (adj.) 🔑, A1
encounter (n.) 🔑 AWL, B1
error (n.) 🔑 AWL, A2
expert (n.) 🔑 AWL, A2
negative (adj.) 🔑 AWL, A2
positive (adj.) 🔑 AWL, A2
sample (n.) 🔑, A2
select (v.) 🔑 AWL, A2
suspicious (adj.) 🔑, B1

UNIT 2

complex (adj.) 🔑 AWL, A2
concentrate (v.) 🔑 AWL, A2
consume (v.) AWL, B1
diet (n.) 🔑, A2
disgusting (adj.) 🔑, B1
distinguish (v.) 🔑, B1
estimate (v.) 🔑 AWL, A2
flavor (n.) 🔑, B1
occasionally (adv.) 🔑, B1
mix (v.) 🔑, A2
mood (n.) 🔑, B1
spicy (adj.) 🔑, B1
swallow (v.) 🔑, B1
trend (n.) 🔑 AWL, A2
wise (adj.) 🔑, B1

UNIT 3

adapt (v.) 🔑 AWL, B1
considerably (adv.) 🔑, B2
cope (v.) 🔑, B1
crisis (n.) 🔑, A2
curious (adj.) 🔑, B1
handle (v.) 🔑, A2
justify (v.) 🔑 AWL, B1
permanent (adj.) 🔑, A2
position (n.) 🔑, B1
research (n.) 🔑 AWL, A2
steady (adj.) 🔑, B1
struggle (v.) 🔑, A2
suffer (v.) 🔑, A1
support (v.) 🔑, B2
unemployed (adj.) 🔑, B1
wages (n.) 🔑, A2

UNIT 4

aimed at (phr.) 🔑, B1
appeal (n.) 🔑, A2
brand (n.) 🔑, B1
campaign (n.) 🔑, A2
claim (v.) 🔑, A1
deliberately (adv.) 🔑, B1
evidence (n.) 🔑 AWL, A1
injury (n.) 🔑 AWL, A2
monitor (v.) 🔑 AWL, B1
persuade (v.) 🔑, A2
regulations (n.) 🔑 AWL, A2
relate to (phr.) 🔑, A1
withdraw (v.) 🔑, A1

UNIT 5

audience (n.) 🔑, A1
discover (v.) 🔑, A1
embarrass (v.) 🔑, B2
expose (v.) 🔑 AWL, B1
financial (adj.) 🔑 AWL, A1
funds (n.) 🔑 AWL, A1
income (n.) 🔑 AWL, A1
invention (n.) 🔑, B2
investigate (v.) 🔑 AWL, A2
locate (v.) 🔑 AWL, B1
model (n.) 🔑, A2
mystery (n.) 🔑, B1
previous (adj.) 🔑 AWL, A1
promote (v.) 🔑 AWL, B1
prove (v.) 🔑, A1
publish (v.) 🔑, A1
reputation (n.) 🔑, B1
retire (v.) 🔑, B1
solve (v.) 🔑, A2
threaten (v.) 🔑, A1

UNIT 6

appropriate (adj.) 🔑 AWL, A1
benefit (n.) 🔑 AWL, A1
consumer (n.) 🔑 AWL, A1
demand (v.) 🔑, B1
fair (adj.) 🔑, A2
guilty (adj.) 🔑, A2
ignore (v.) 🔑 AWL, A1
impact (n.) 🔑 AWL, B1
influence (v.) 🔑, A2
lie (v.) 🔑, A1

profit (n.) 🔑, A1
sensible (adj.) 🔑, B1
trust (v.) 🔑, A2

UNIT 7

acquire (v.) 🔑 AWL, A2
analysis (n.) 🔑 AWL, A1
associated with (adj.) 🔑, B2
circumstances (n.) 🔑 AWL, A2
complicated (adj.) 🔑, B1
conduct (v.) 🔑 AWL, A2
demonstrate (v.) 🔑 AWL, A2
dramatic (adj.) 🔑 AWL, B1
immediate (adj.) 🔑, A2
independence (n.) 🔑, A2
outcome (n.) AWL, A2
pleasure (n.) 🔑, A2
somewhat (adv.) 🔑 AWL, A2

UNIT 8

achieve (v.) 🔑 AWL, A1
determination (n.) 🔑, B1
develop (v.) 🔑, B1
emphasize (v.) 🔑 AWL, A2
fear (v.) 🔑, A2
goal (n.) 🔑 AWL, A2
lack (v.) 🔑, B1
measure (v.) 🔑, A1
permit (v.) 🔑, A2
preparation (n.) 🔑, A2
realistic (adj.) 🔑, B2
ruin (v.) 🔑, B2
status (n.) 🔑 AWL, A1
top (adj.) 🔑, A2